To Yvonne

With love

[signature] Packham

20.05.10

YORKSHIRE
IN WATERCOLOUR

LES PACKHAM

Published by Northern Arts Publications
an imprint of Jeremy Mills Publishing Limited
www.jeremymillspublishing.co.uk

First published 2010

Paperback
ISBN: 978-1-906600-48-8

Hardback
ISBN: 978-1-906600-50-1

Special Edition
ISBN: 978-1-906600-51-8

FRONTISPIECE

BOLTON ABBEY

THE STRID IN Bolton Woods, a couple of miles walk north of Bolton Priory is where the river Wharfe is forced through a narrow channel no more than six or seven feet wide. When standing on the edge observing the boiling waters beneath one feels an almost overwhelming compulsion to jump what appears to be a very short distance to the other side. Many have tried and several have died in their attempt to prove a point. This time I played it safe and captured the Strid at its best.

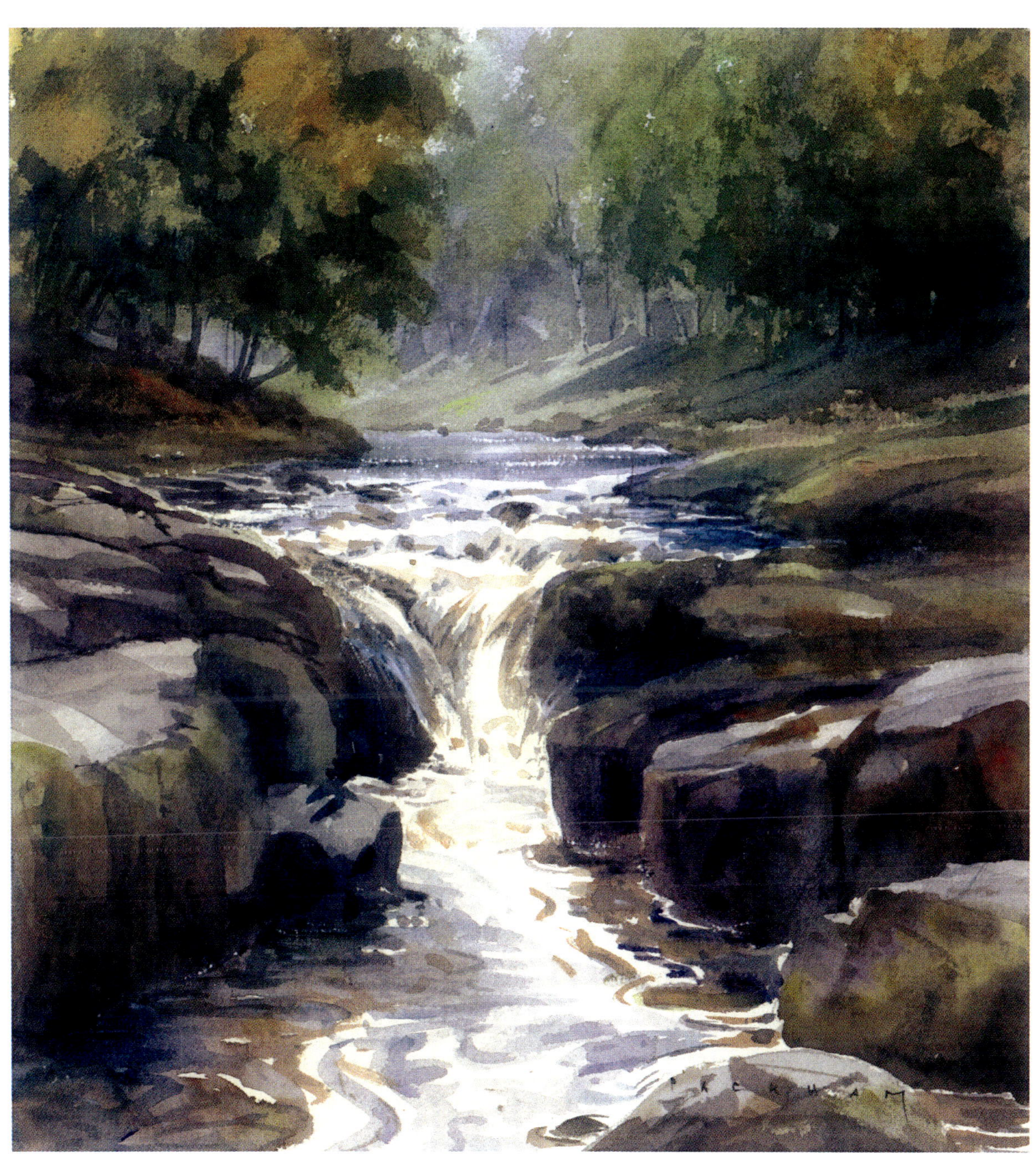
PECKHAM

ACKNOWLEDGEMENTS

ANY BOOK IS never the work of one person and so it is with this small volume. However, this work would never have appeared without the faith of the publisher Jeremy Mills and his dedicated team. Thanks are also due to John Gardner Photography and Day Night Print for photographing and scanning the images; Holly West for research, Allan Darwell for his expertise and advice over the years and to Nature for providing such a rich, inspiring and diverse canvas to copy.

NOTE FROM THE PUBLISHER

I FIRST MET Les Packham and his wife Judy in 2003 when we were involved in a very different publishing project and whilst discussing this I was offered the opportunity to visit his studio and view many of his paintings. It was first time I had seen Les Packham's work. As an amateur watercolourist and publisher of art books, it took me only a very short time to realise that what I had seen were truly exceptional watercolours, the work of a man whose considerable artistic skills were in complete harmony with his landscape.

Back in 2003, I mooted that we might think about producing a book of his paintings in the future, but due to the immense amount of work involved, there the idea lay for over six years until by chance we spoke again and revisited the idea. From then on, the project assumed a greater urgency and we started to discuss the concept, format and design of a book in more detail. We agreed that the format should encompass Les's recent work and be representative of both the life and landscape of Yorkshire, depicting the coastal areas, the Dales, the Moors, villages and towns, paying homage to tradition and heritage whilst accurately recording life in rural Yorkshire as it is lived today.

Les Packham's chosen works for this unique volume show an artist at the zenith of his powers, whose fluid, feather light touches combine with his uncanny understanding of colour to evoke a vision of Yorkshire that each of us will treasure.

JEREMY MILLS
Publisher

DEDICATION

WITH LOVE AND grateful thanks to my dear wife Judith for all her support and understanding over the years.

Also to the memory of Stanley and all our other faithful canines for sharing my adventures.

FOREWORD

I HAVE KNOWN Les Packham for almost twenty years and have always admired his popular style of painting which, for me, epitomises both the character and qualities of the places that inspire his work.

I have been, as head of the Art Department at Tennants Auctioneers in the Dales, associated with many of the painters who have worked in Yorkshire during the 19th and early 20th centuries. I have long felt that Les Packham's work reflects the style and traditions of such great artists from the Wharfedale and Staithes groups as Arthur Reginald Smith, Bertram Priestman, Reginald Grange Brundrit and Rowland Henry Hill.

Les's long and prolific career and his kinship with other members of the Yorkshire painting fraternity have influenced a new generation of aspiring painters who will, hopefully, continue to capture the Yorkshire scene in all it's changing moods. A landscape that remains so beloved by generations of artists, poets and connoisseurs of the 'Northern genre'.

ALLAN DARWELL
Head of Art, Tennants Autioneers
Leyburn

ARNCLIFFE

LITTONDALE IS A tributary dale of upper Wharfedale and its principal village is Arncliffe. The old name for Littondale is Amerdale – the model for the television serial *Emmerdale*. In fact, early filming for the series took place in Arncliffe.

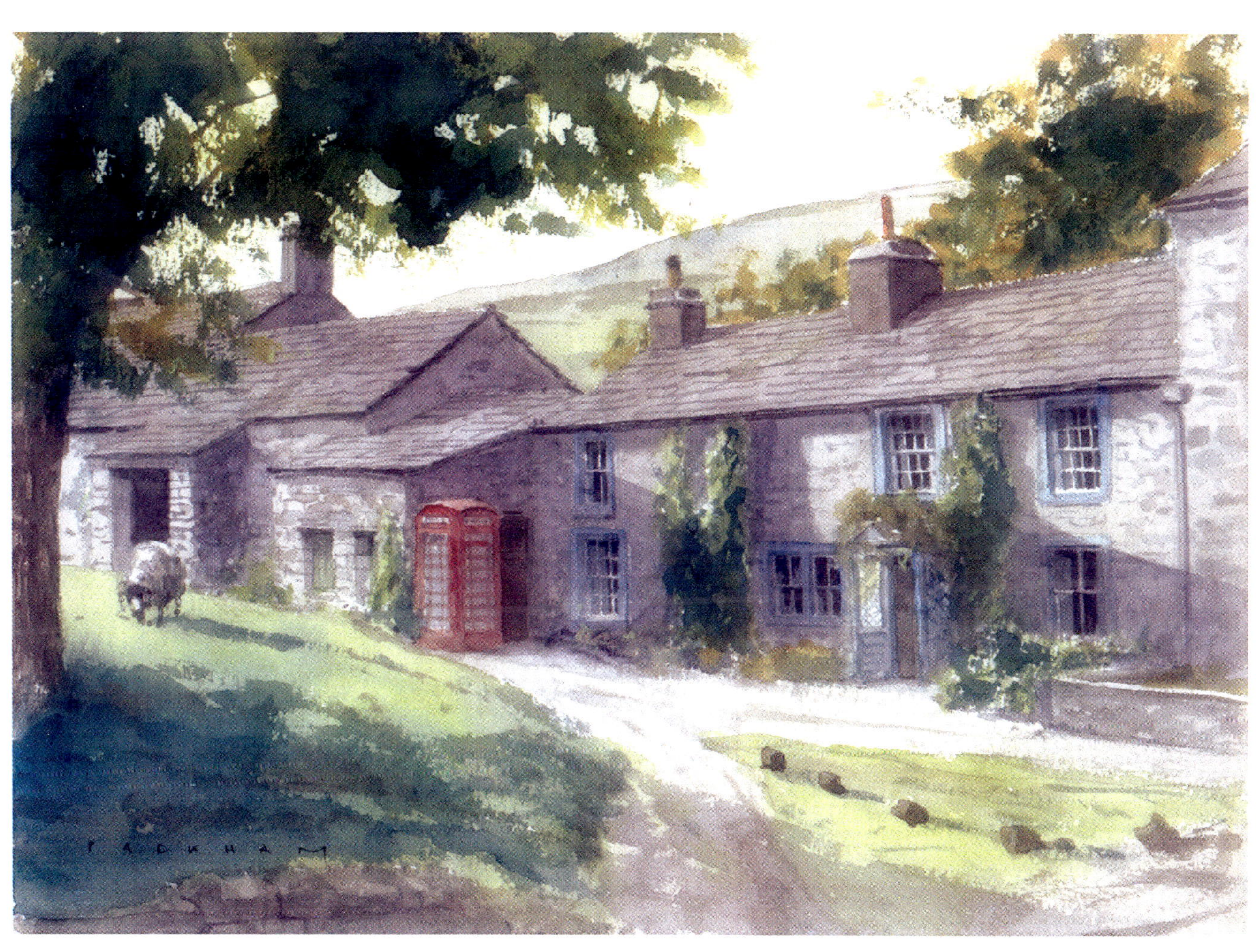
PACKHAM

BAILDON MOOR

BRACKEN HALL FARM is now an education centre on Baildon Moor, overlooking Shipley Glen. As a small boy it was a favourite place to visit on a Sunday afternoon, usually combined with a trip either up or down the Victorian Glen Tramway.

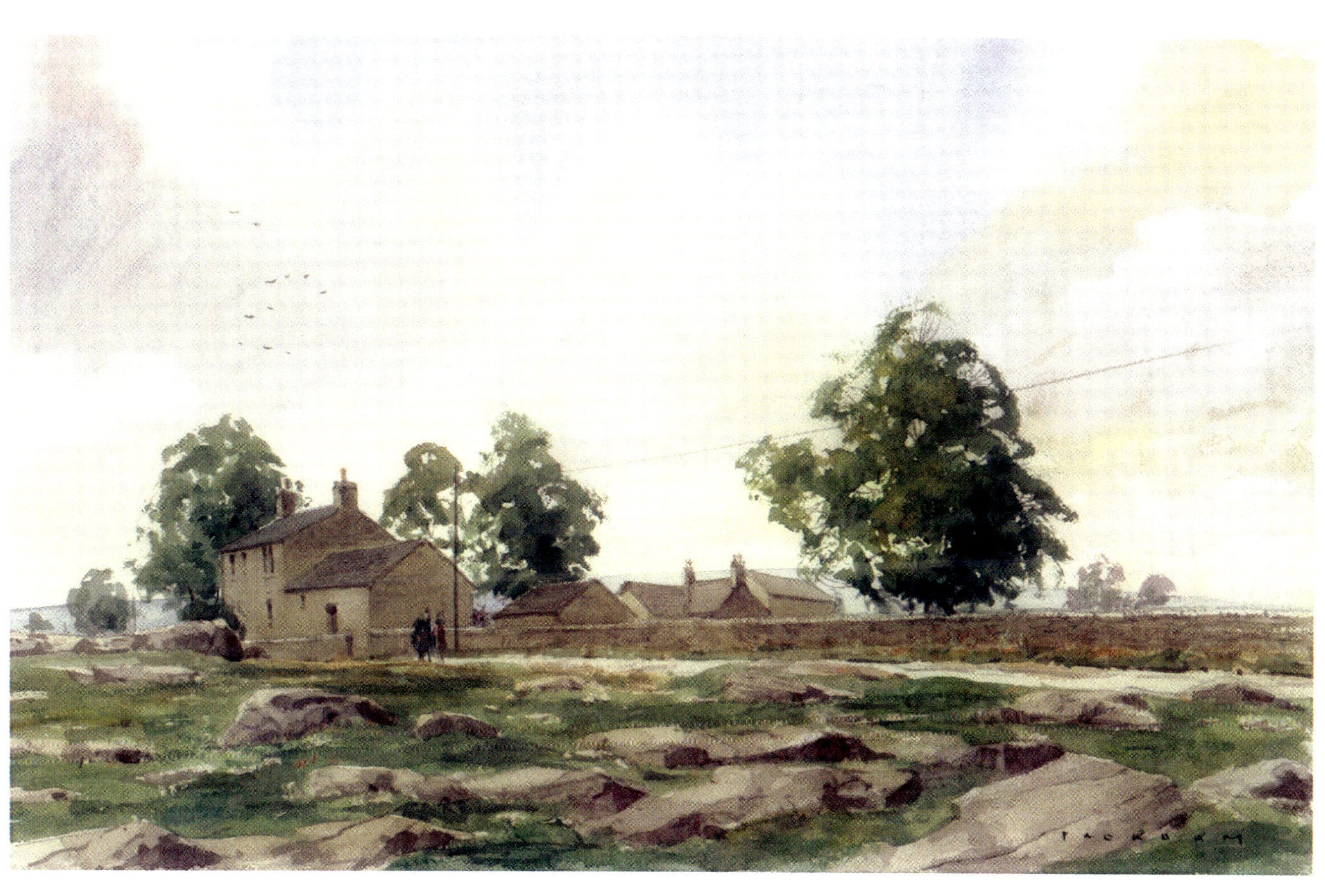

KELD

KELD IS A small hamlet at the head of Swaledale which consists of a few cottages, a couple of chapels, a school and a youth hostel huddled round a small square – it is exceptionally good walking country.

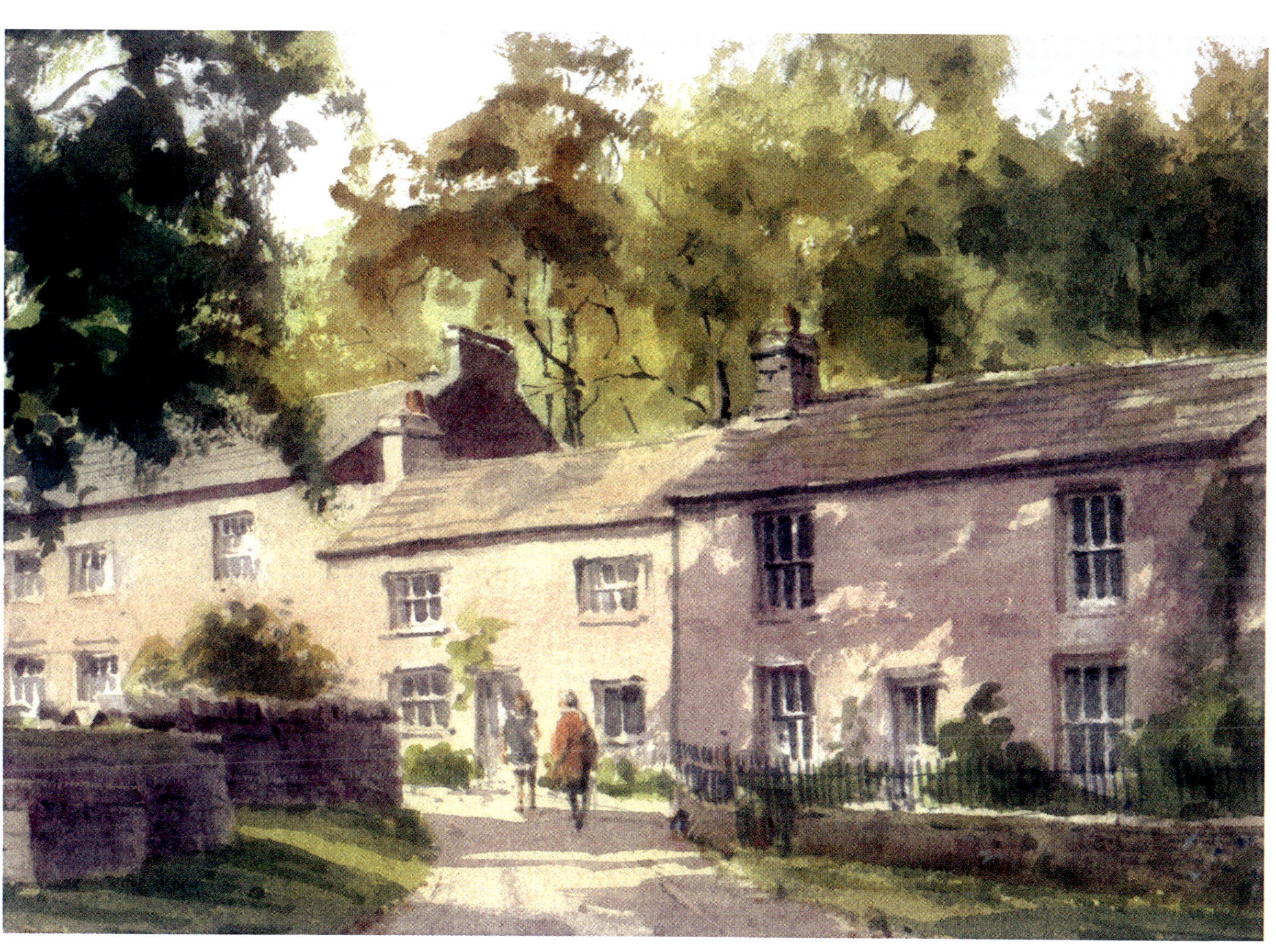

BAINTON

BAINTON IS AN attractive village in the Wolds quite close to Driffield and because I particularly liked the view I decided on this composition which highlights the church tower above the nestling cottages.

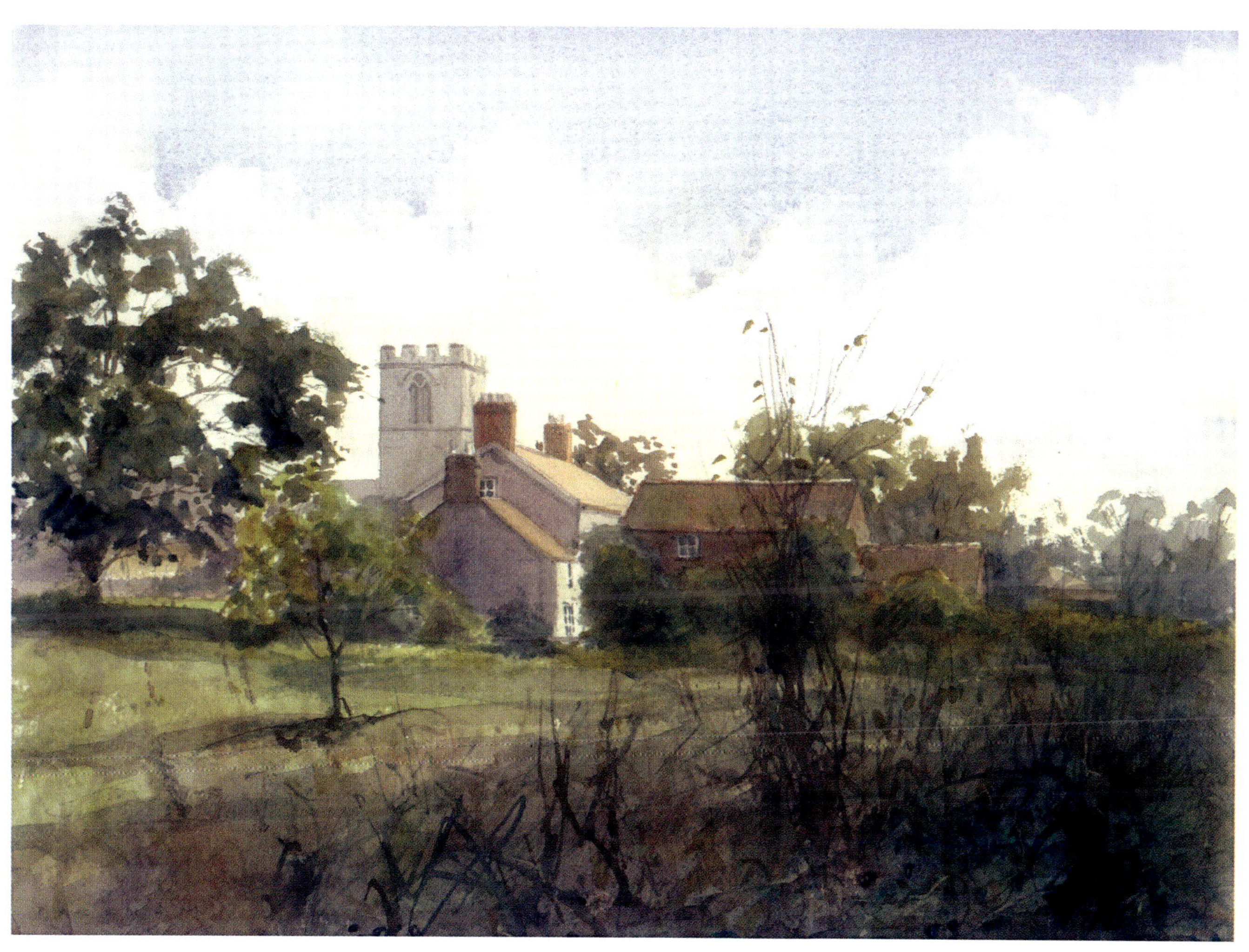

THWAITE

A PARTICULAR FAVOURITE of mine is Swaledale so I thoroughly enjoyed this composition of cottages in summer time – what a cracking little subject!

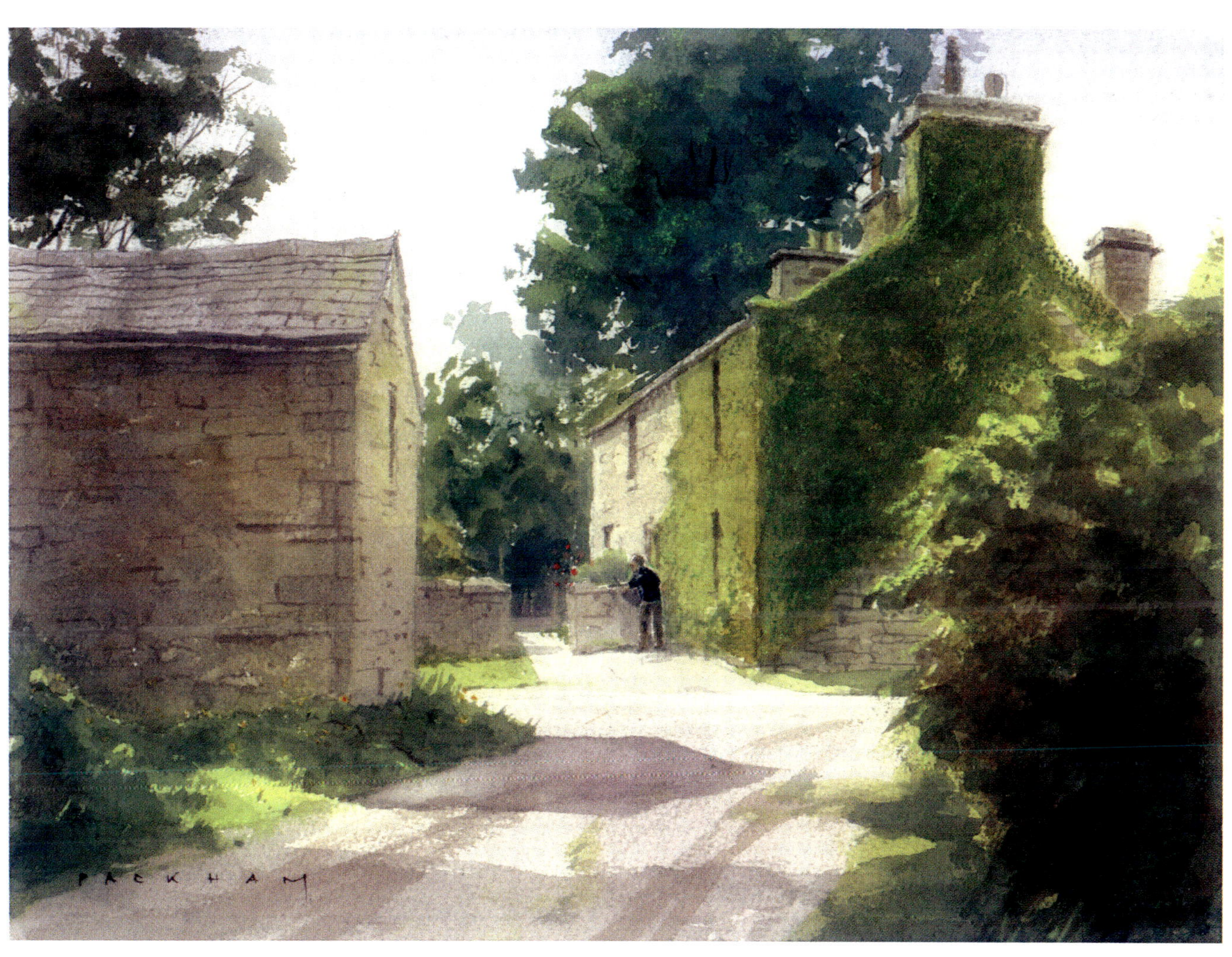
PACKHAM

BISHOPDALE

BISHOPDALE LIES BETWEEN upper Wharfedale and Wensleydale and is unusual in its NE/SW trajectory. This view comes almost as a surprise as one travels north east from Cray over Kidstones Pass towards Leyburn. It delights me every time.

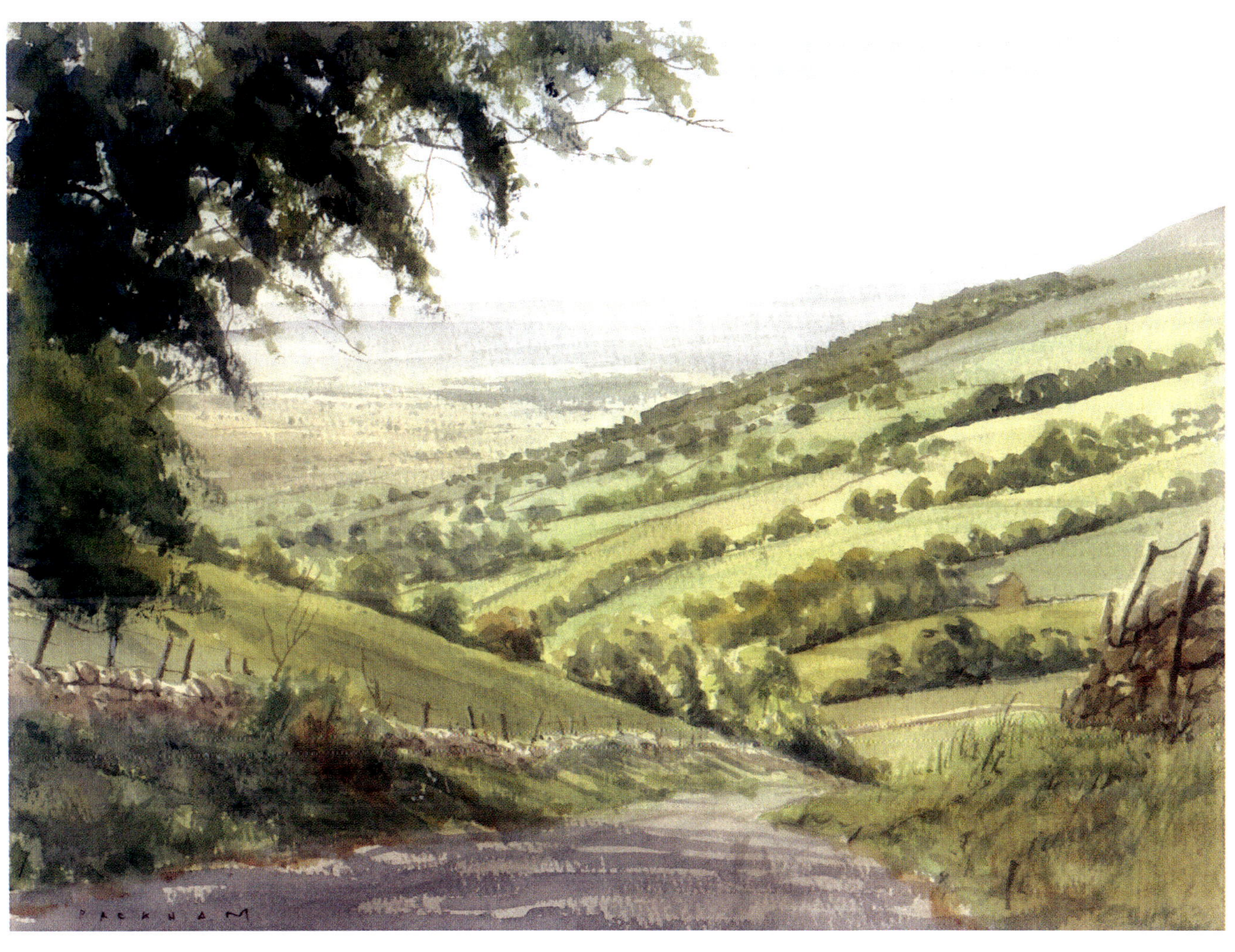
PECKHAM

BRIDLINGTON

AFTER A FINE fish lunch on a warm summer's day I was suddenly struck by the sharp sunlight and shadows on these two fishing boats in Bridlington harbour. Looking directly into the sun the intriguing effects made by the light on the wet mud made a challenging subject.

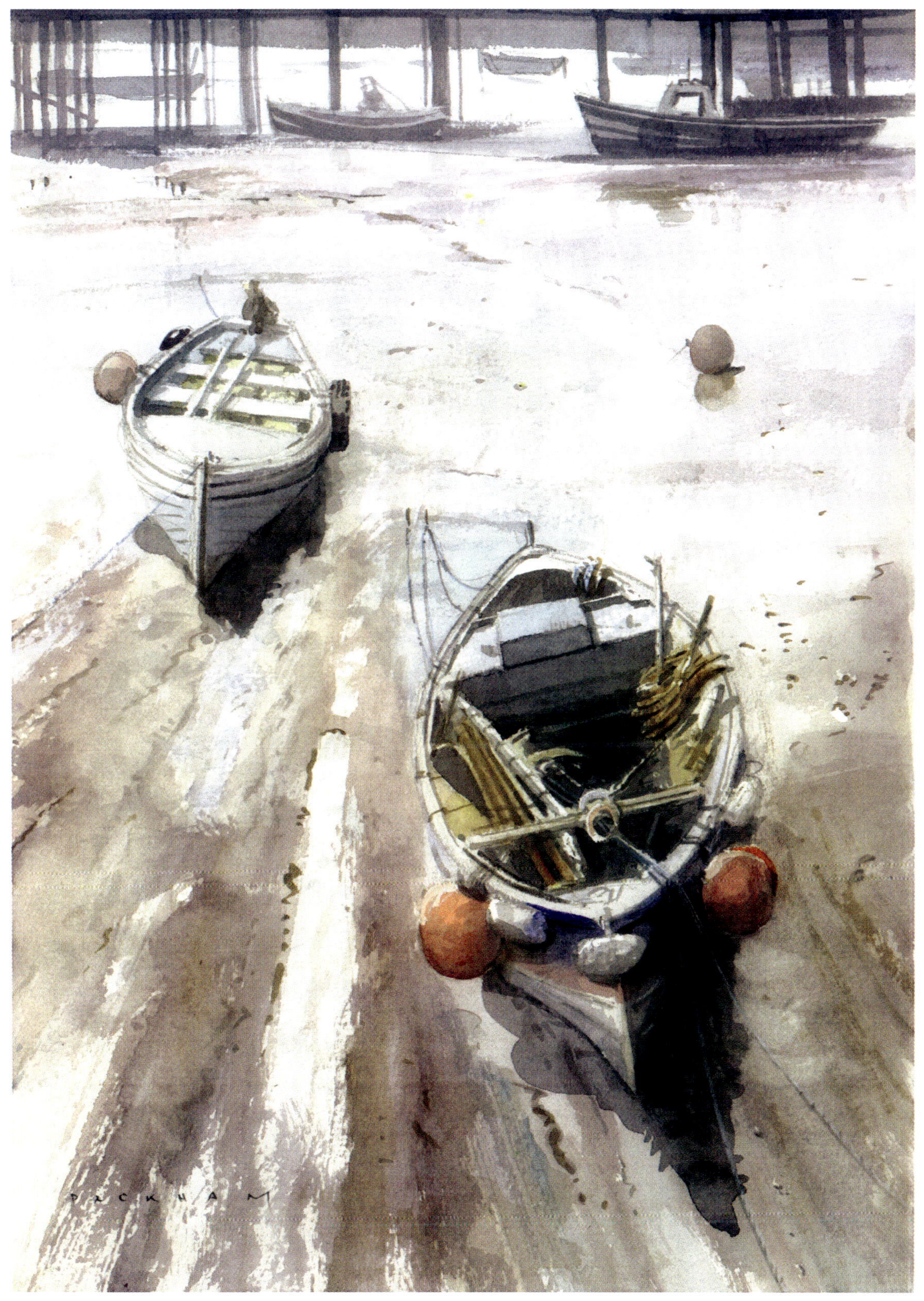
PACKHAM

STAITHES

BOULBY CLIFFS, AT nearly 600 feet, are the highest in England. This view, painted on a winter's day from Staithes, shows the extreme edge of Cowbar Nab which helps protect the harbour from the harsh northerly winds which predominate at this time of year.

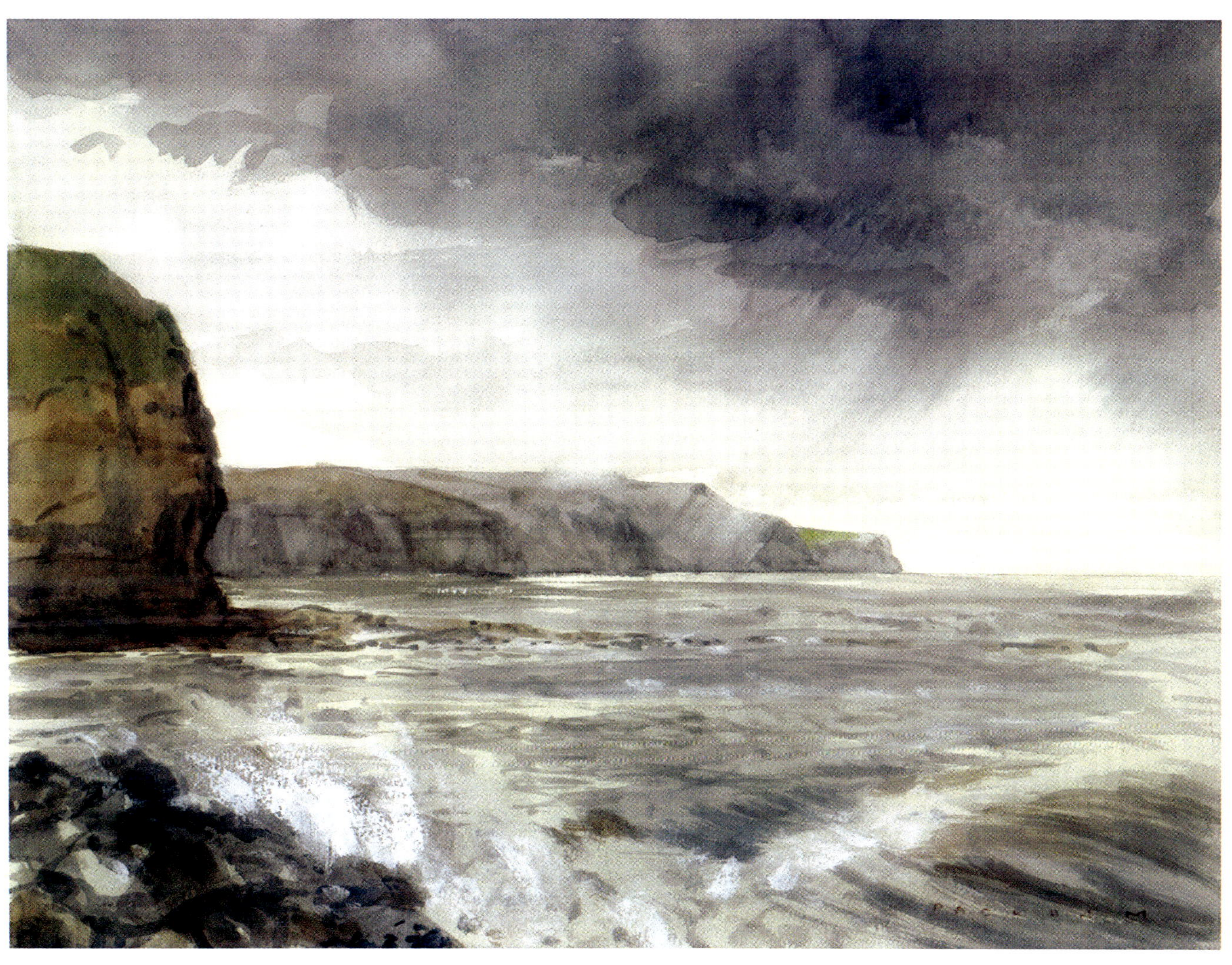

HAWORTH MOOR

THIS VIEW, LOOKING up at a derelict Top Withens Farm, said to be the area which inspired Emily Brontë's *Wuthering Heights*, is how I remember it as a boy when I would go walking there with a favourite uncle. Top Withens has now been capped but Haworth Moor is still one of my favourite painting places.

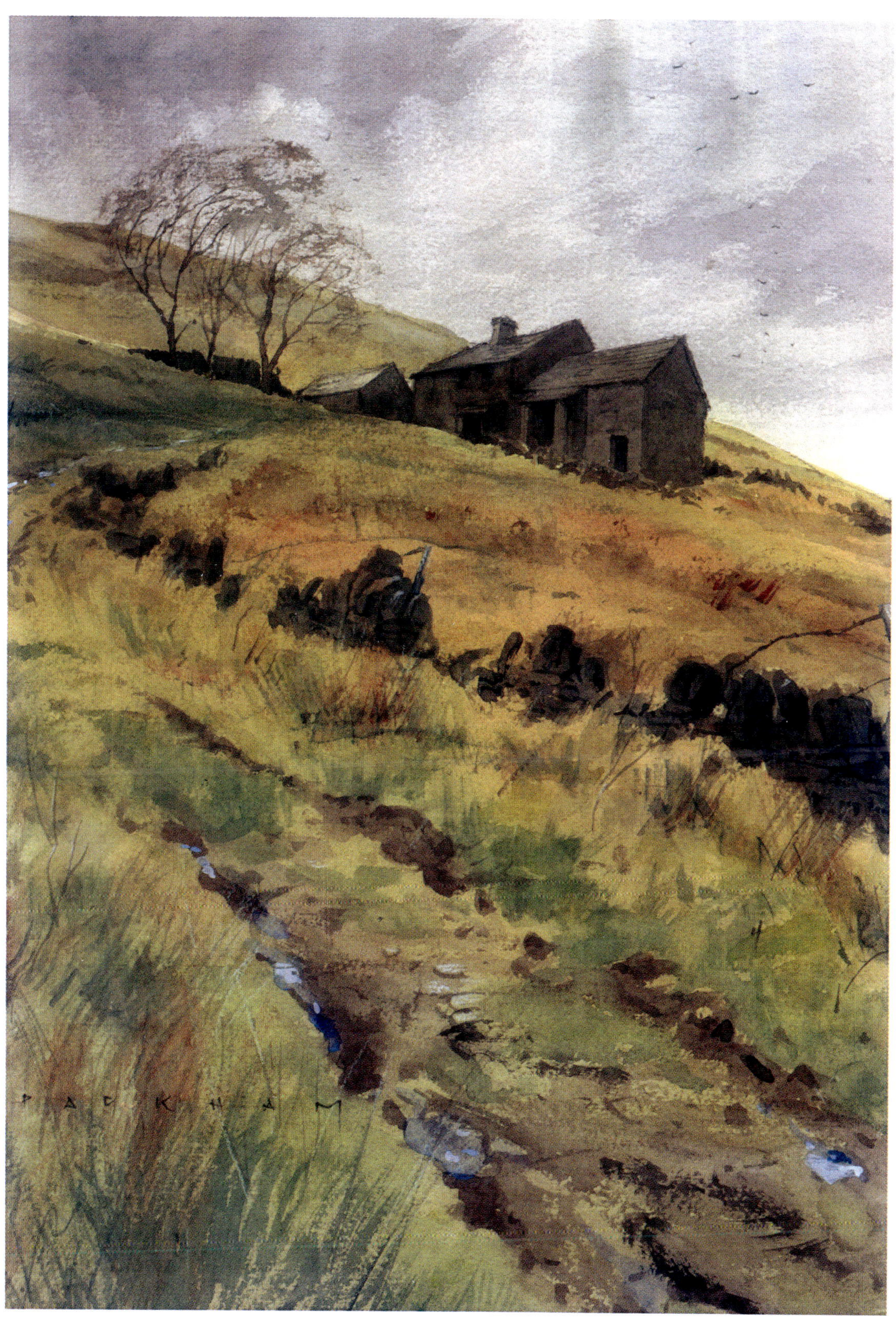
P A C K H A M

HOVINGHAM

HOVINGHAM BOASTS MANY fine houses including Hovingham Hall, home of the Worsley family, and an interesting church with a Saxon tower. However, I was attracted to these cottages just off the main street because they made a pleasingly different subject.

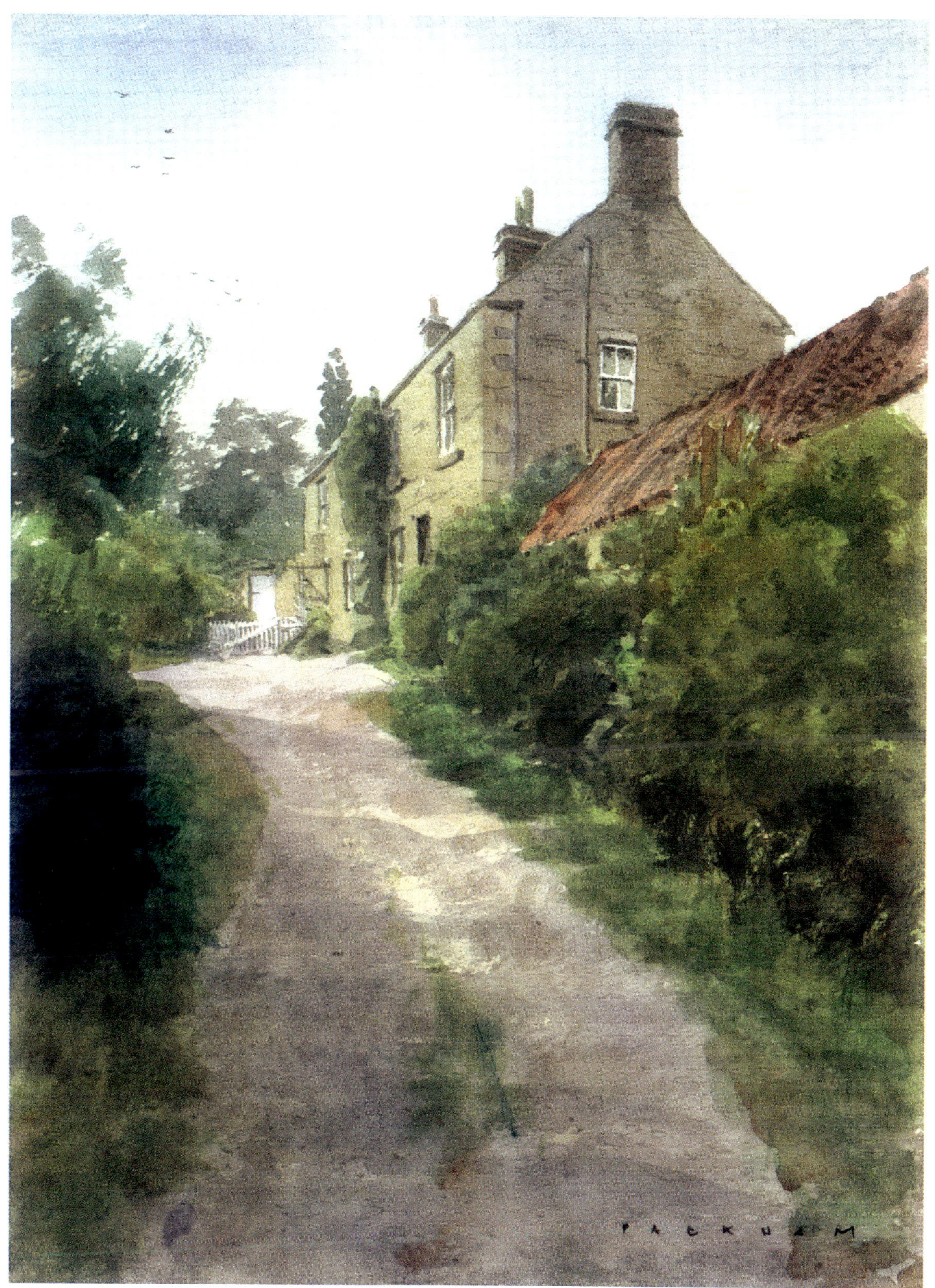

WHITBY

THIS IMAGE HAS been seen before. But I feel it's a sufficiently unusual view of the harbour to be reproduced again. It shows some of the sizeable ships that journey up the river Esk and portrays the industrial side of Whitby.

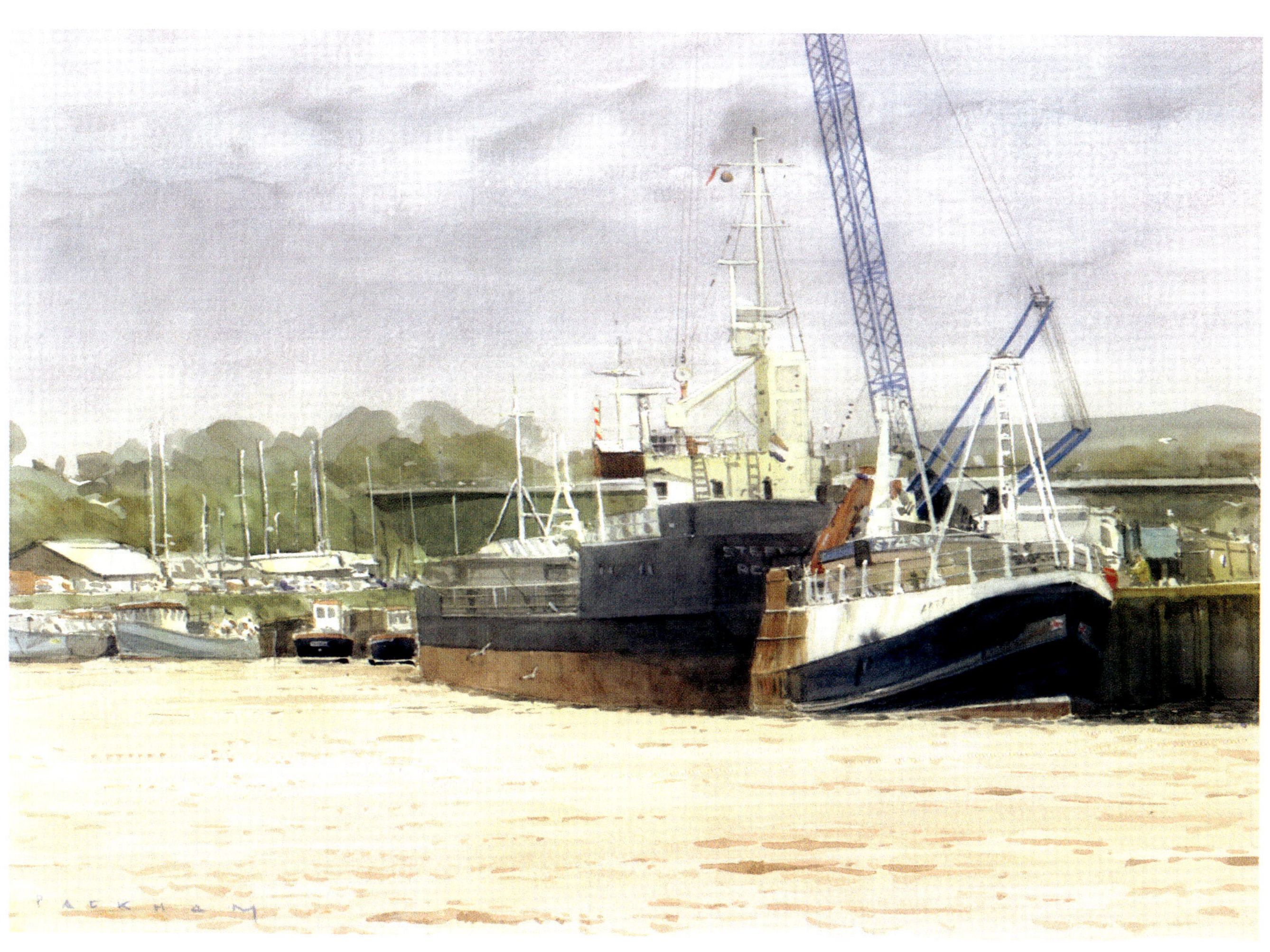
PACKHAM

HADE EDGE

I WAS ATTRACTED by the view from this typically Yorkshire farm track in this moorland village which lies between Holmfirth and Dunford Bridge.

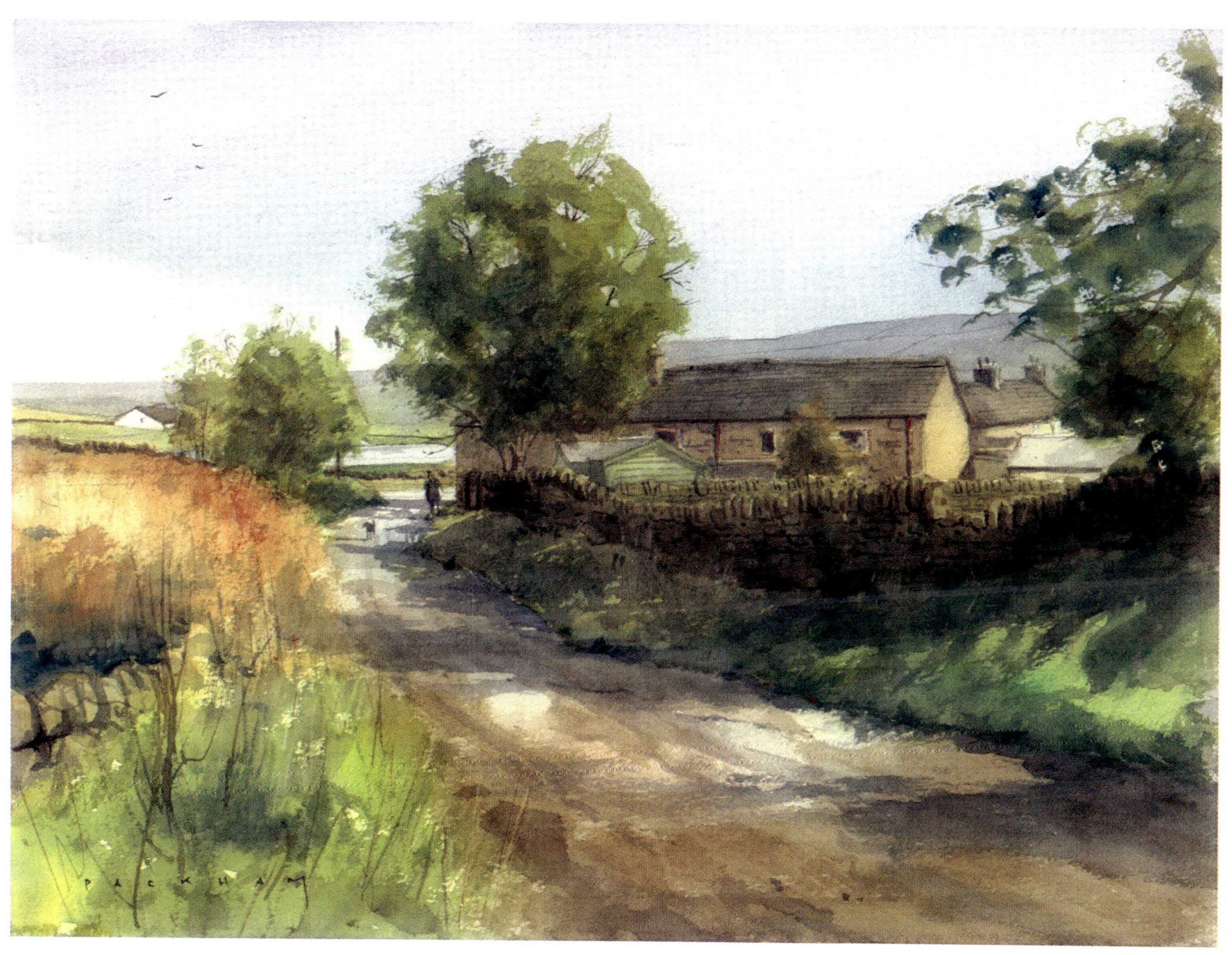
PACKHAM

RAMSGILL

NIDDERDALE IS PROBABLY the most verdant and in the past one of the most industrialised of the Yorkshire Dales. Travelling from Pateley Bridge to the head of the dale at the Angram and Scar House reservoirs, Ramsgill lies about half way at the northern edge of Gouthwaite Reservoir. The very flat light on the day of this painting is apparent.

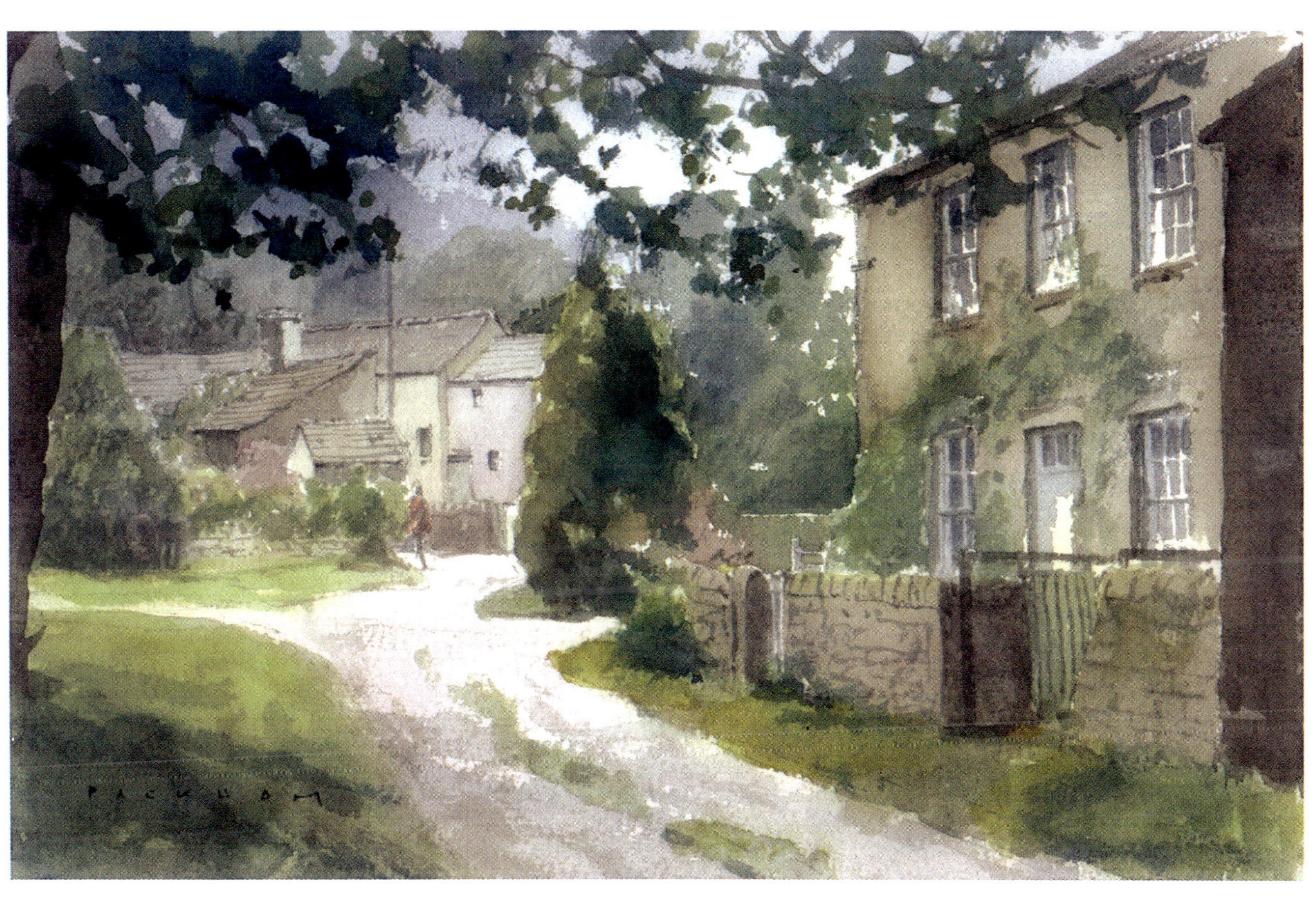

BECKWITHSHAW

BECKWITHSHAW, A VILLAGE between Otley and Harrogate, is interesting with much to be seen in the way of wildlife. Beaver Dyke Reservior shown here in Spring gives a glimpse of the bright colours that emerge after a dreary winter.

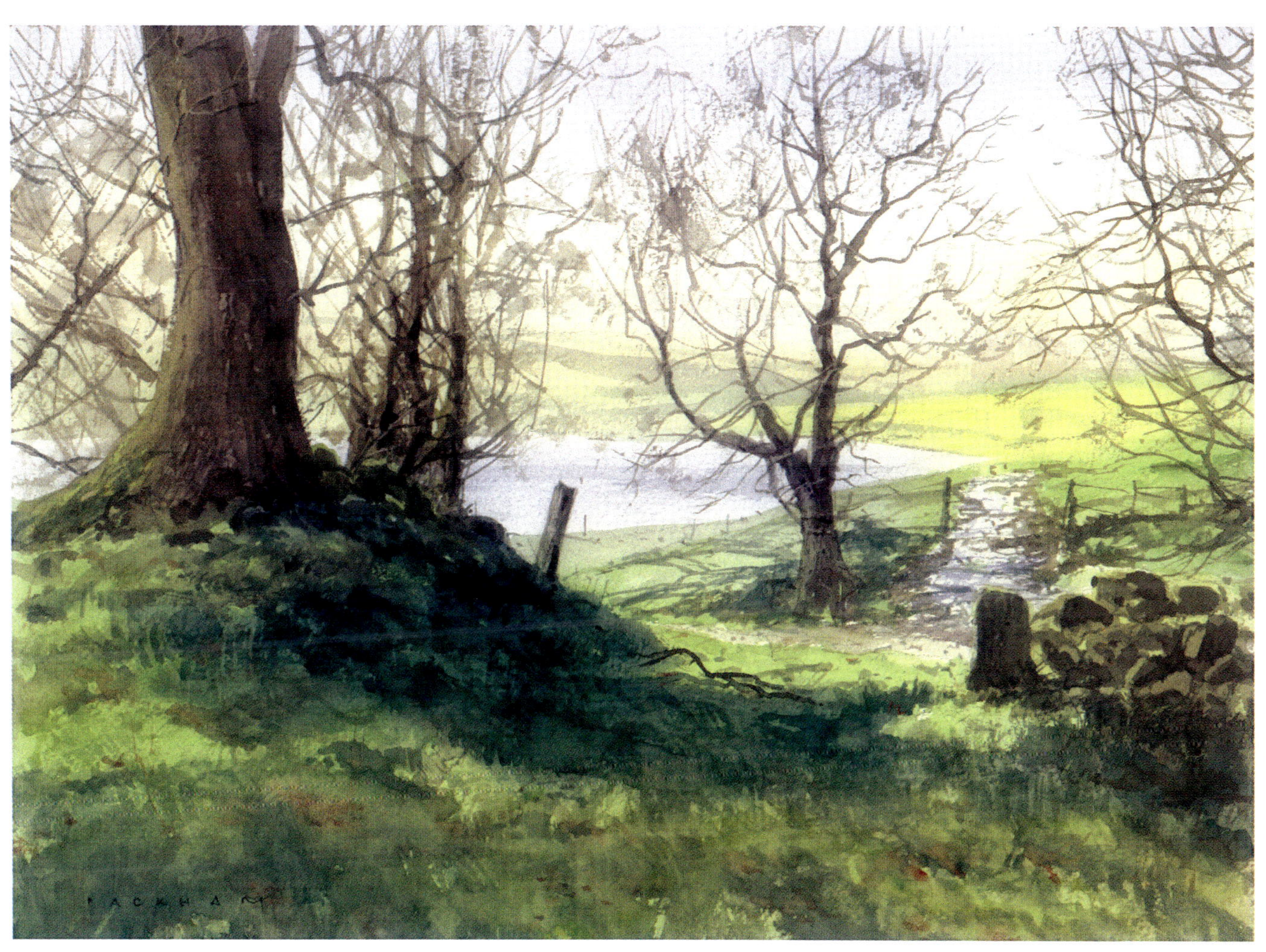

SMALL BANKS

YORKSHIRE HILLSIDES ARE riddled with good solid built barns like this one at Small Banks, a moorland community close to Addingham. There is something I find appealing about barns and the solid reliability they exude.

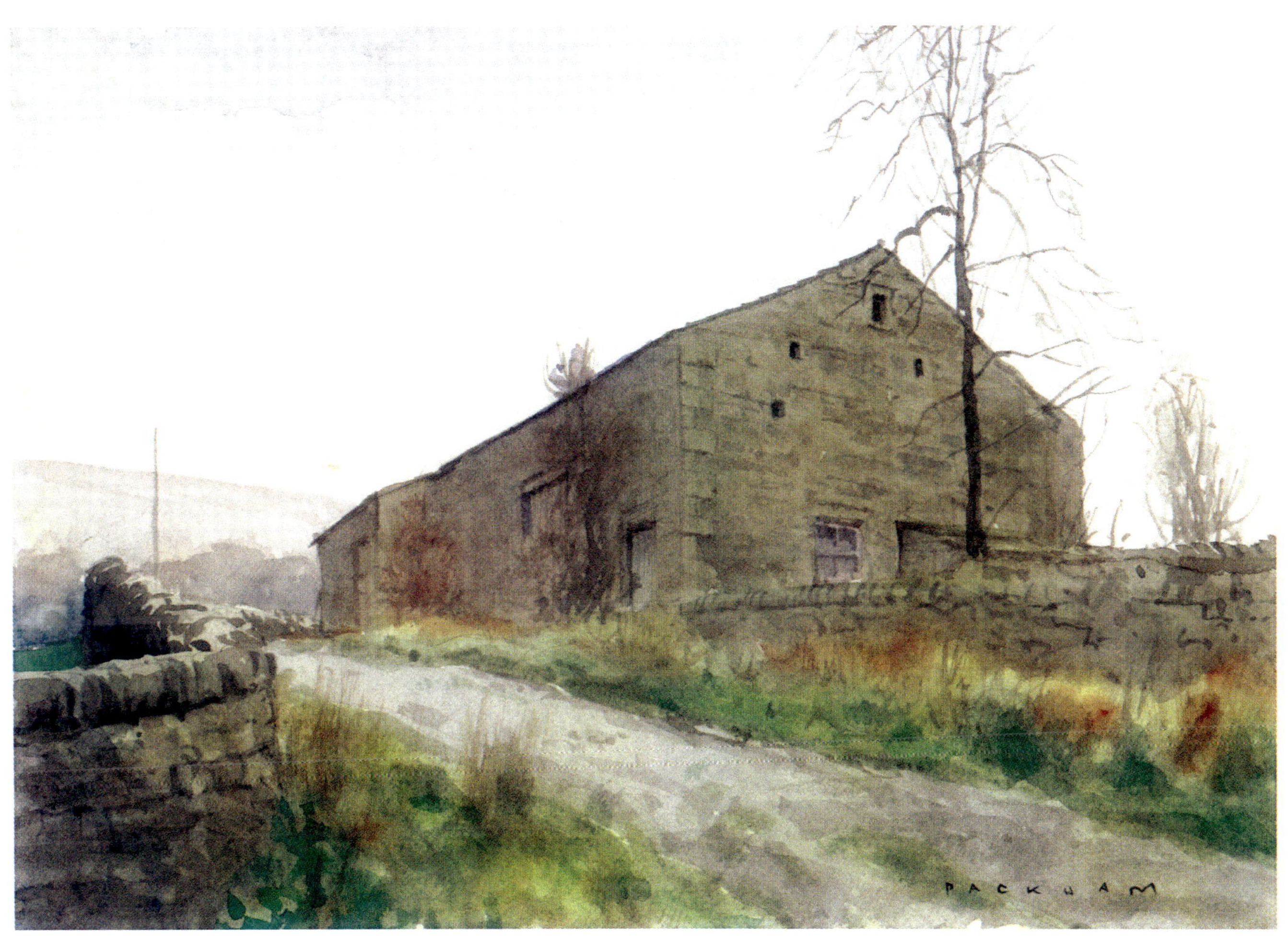
PACKHAM

HADE EDGE

HADE EDGE ABOVE Holmfirth is shown again in this view, this time in early summer with its myriad greens. This is a lovely area and a walk around one of the reservoirs approached from Clough Foot Lane is a must on a warm summer's day.

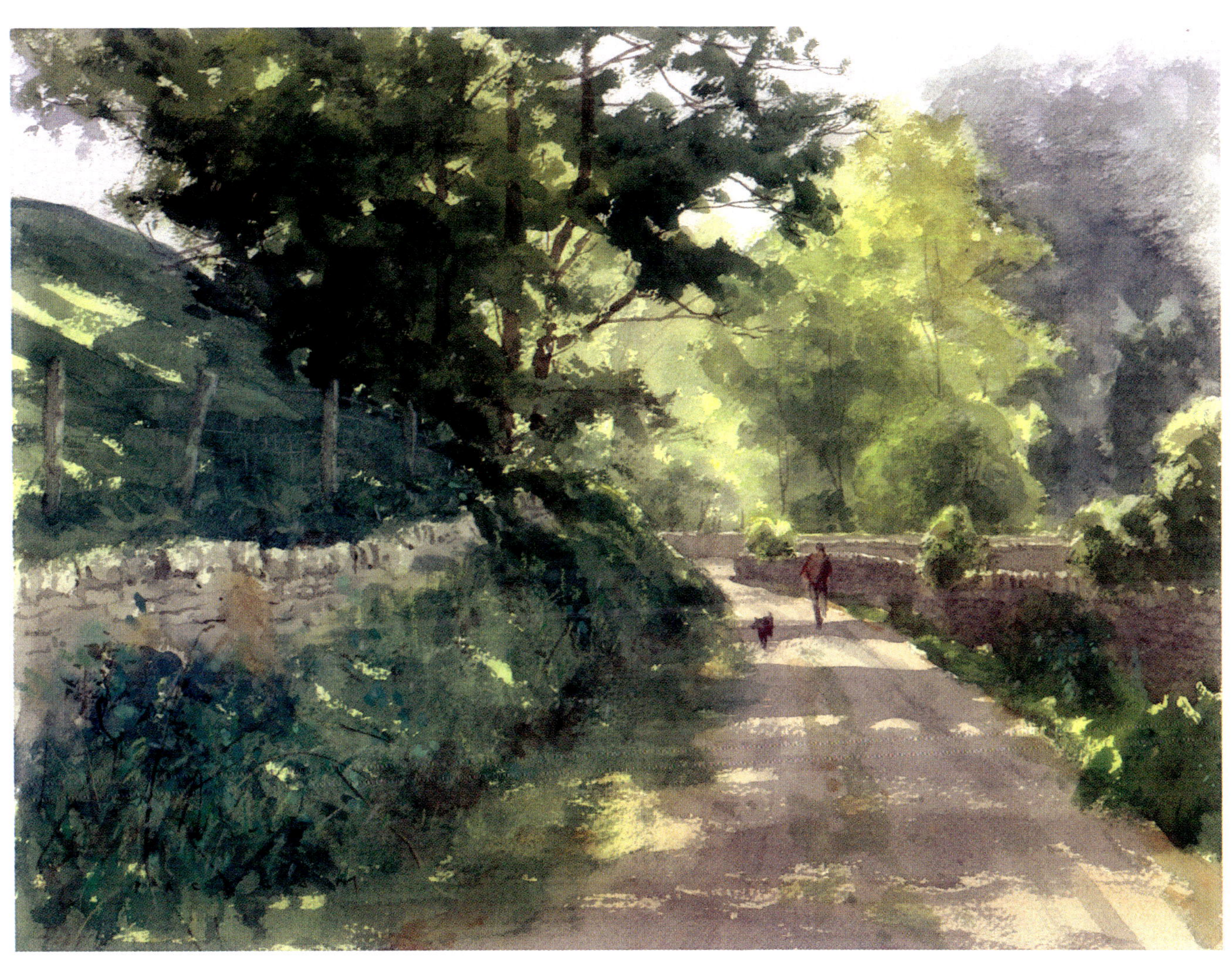

STAITHES

STAITHES IS A fascinating place to paint. Once full of fishing cobles such as this, the numbers are dwindling due to the decline in the fishing industry.

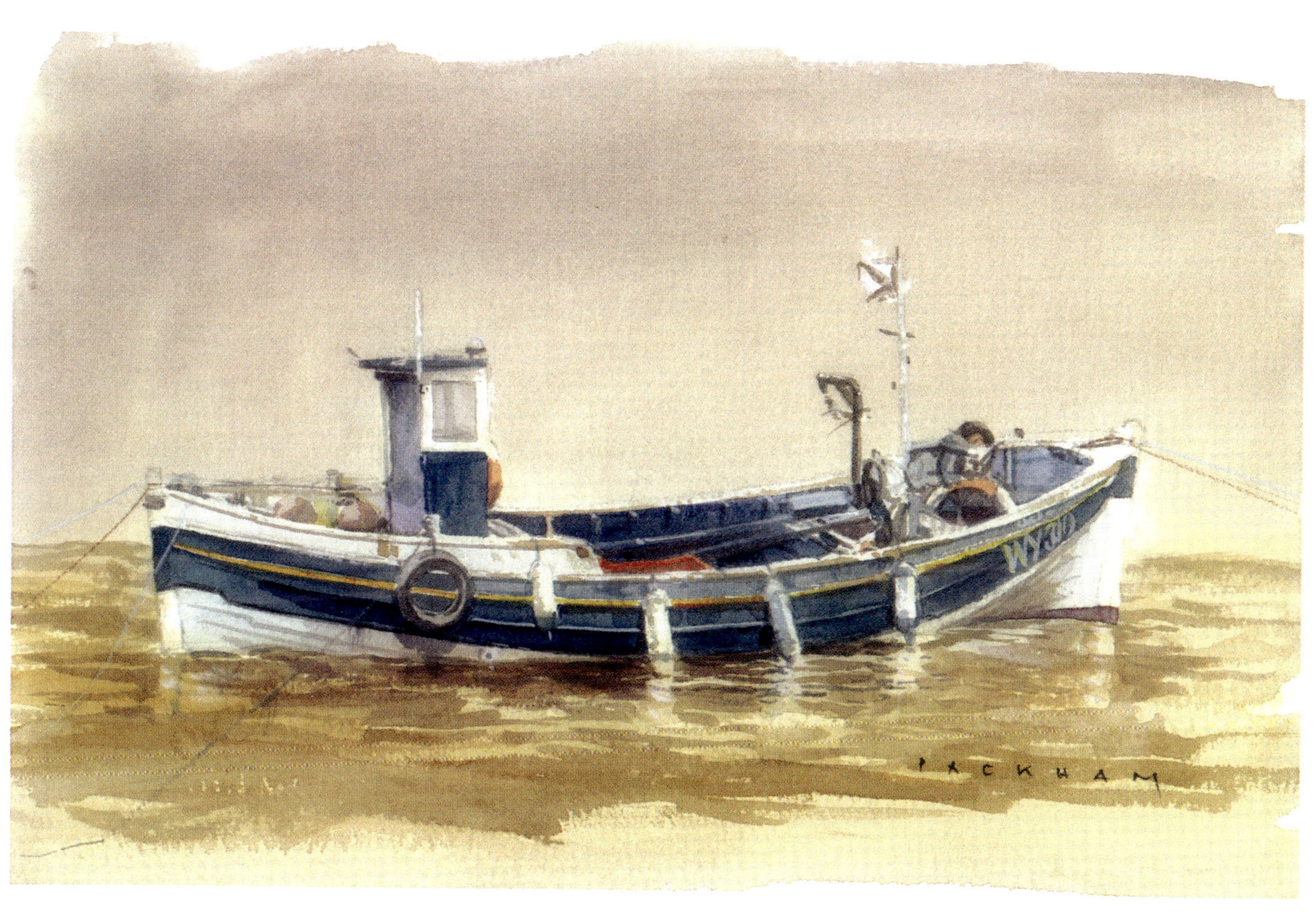
PACKHAM

FOLLIFOOT

FOLLIFOOT IS SITUATED just south of Harrogate and is almost entirely built of Yorkshire stone. It provides many a subject to paint and here the Radcliffe Arms and the Old Blacksmith's Cottage are featured.

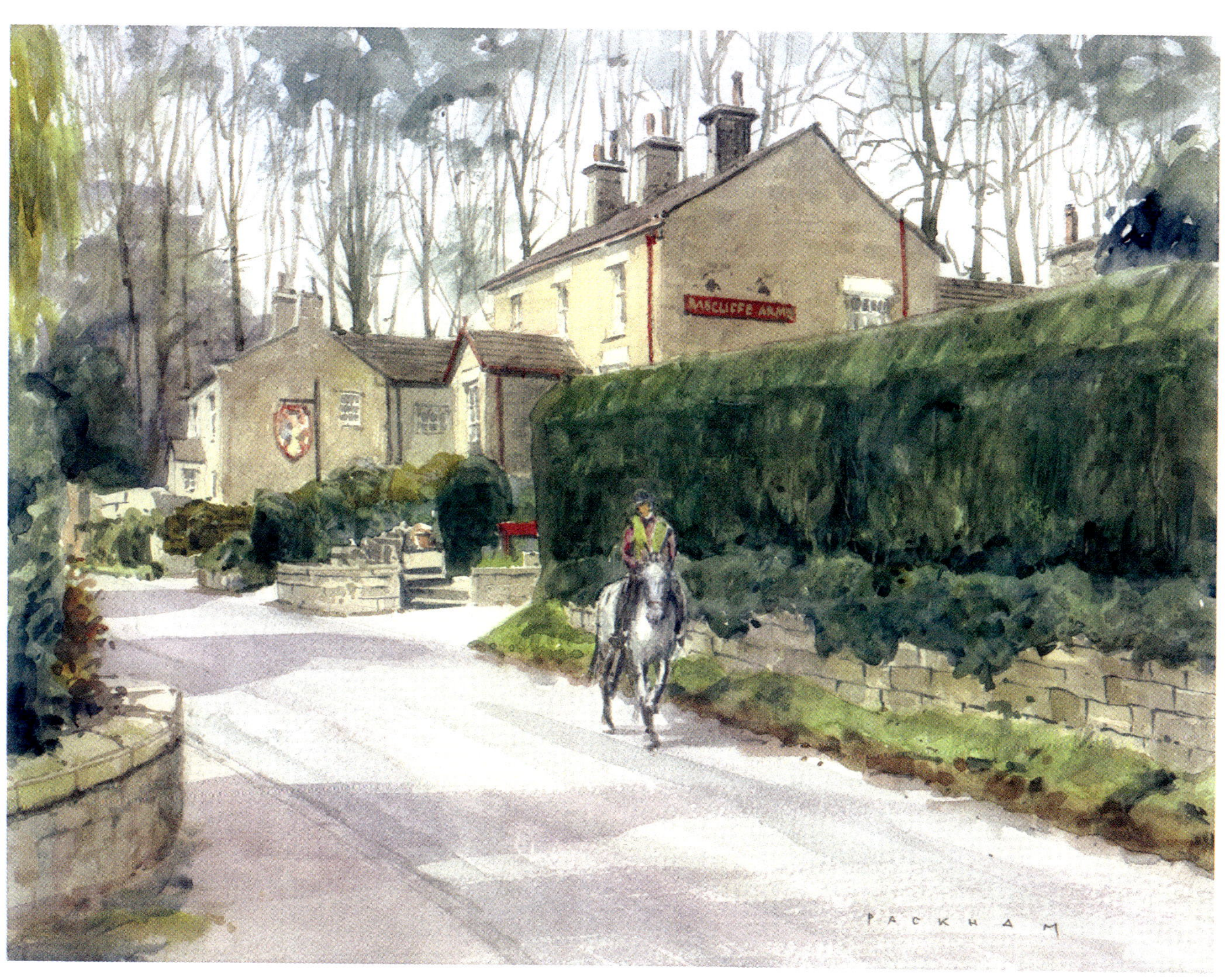
PACKHAM

RIPON

FOUNTAINS ABBEY NEAR the city of Ripon was founded in the twelfth century by the Cistercian Monks. This impressive ruin is set in a beautiful green valley at the side of the river Skell.

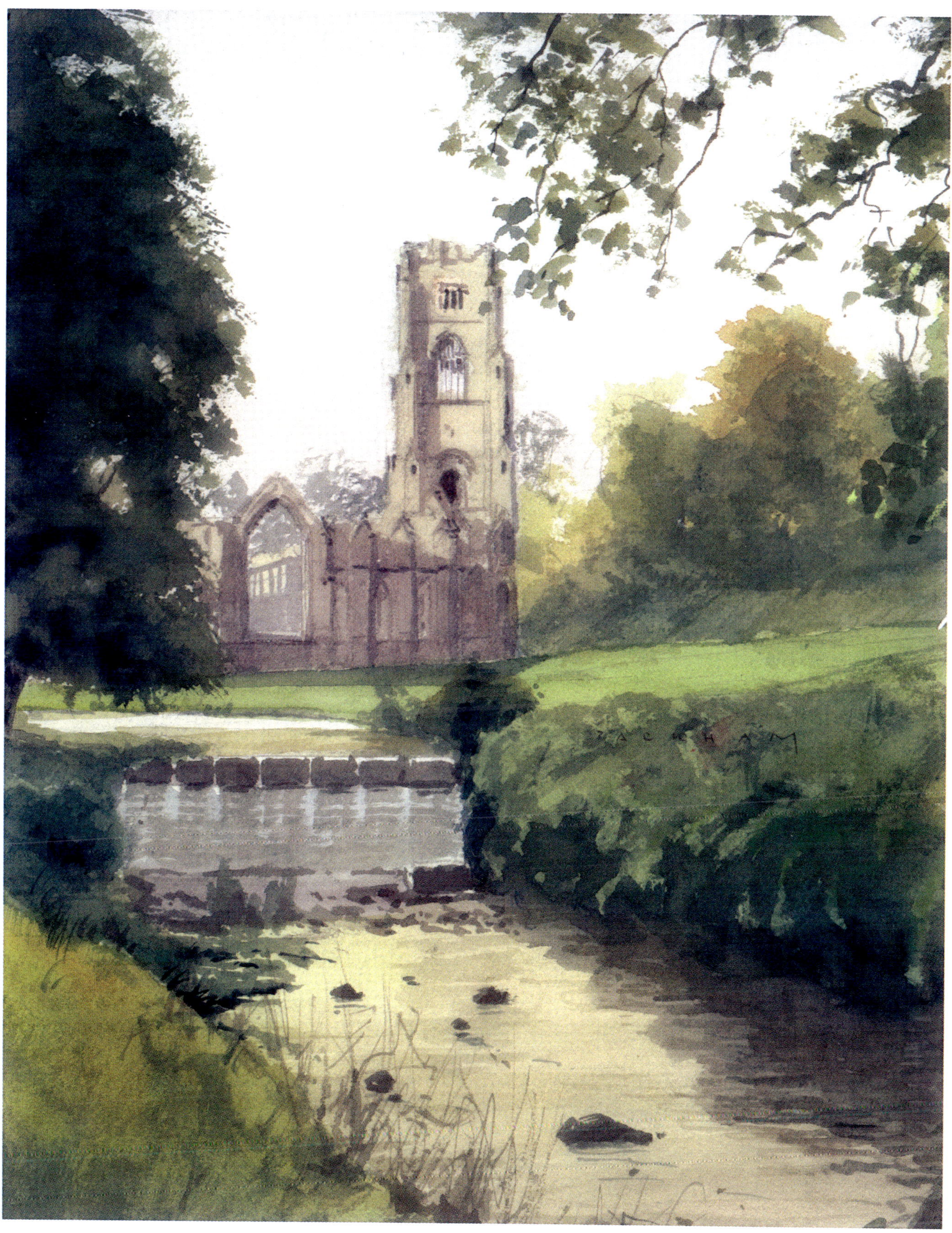

HARROGATE

A LITTLE STUDY of three judges making up their minds about the pig exhibits at the Great Yorkshire Show.

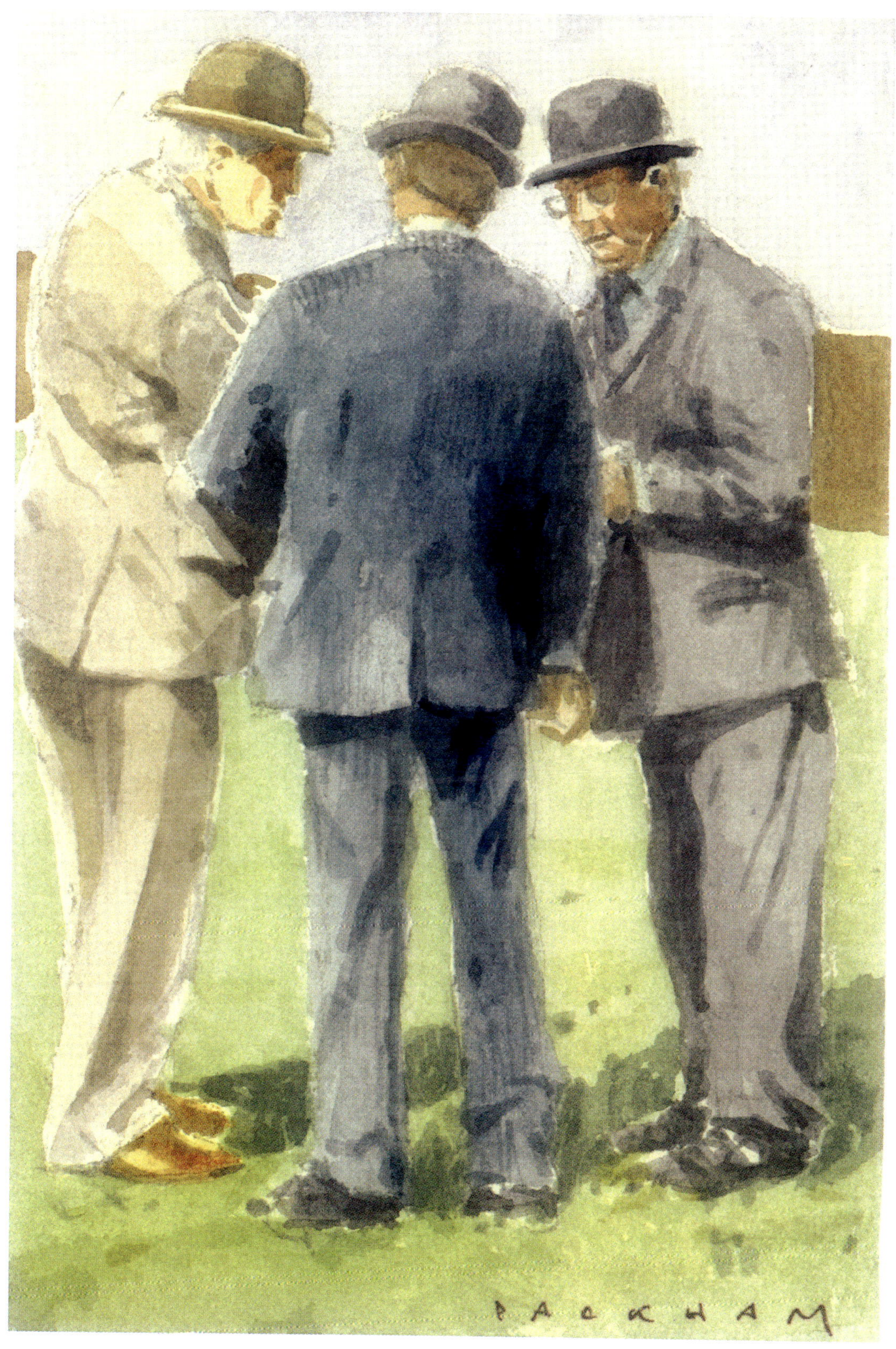
PACKHAM

HAWORTH
MOOR

THIS STONE BRIDGE over a moorland beck on Haworth moor was known to be a favourite spot of the Brontë sisters and has subsequently been named after them.

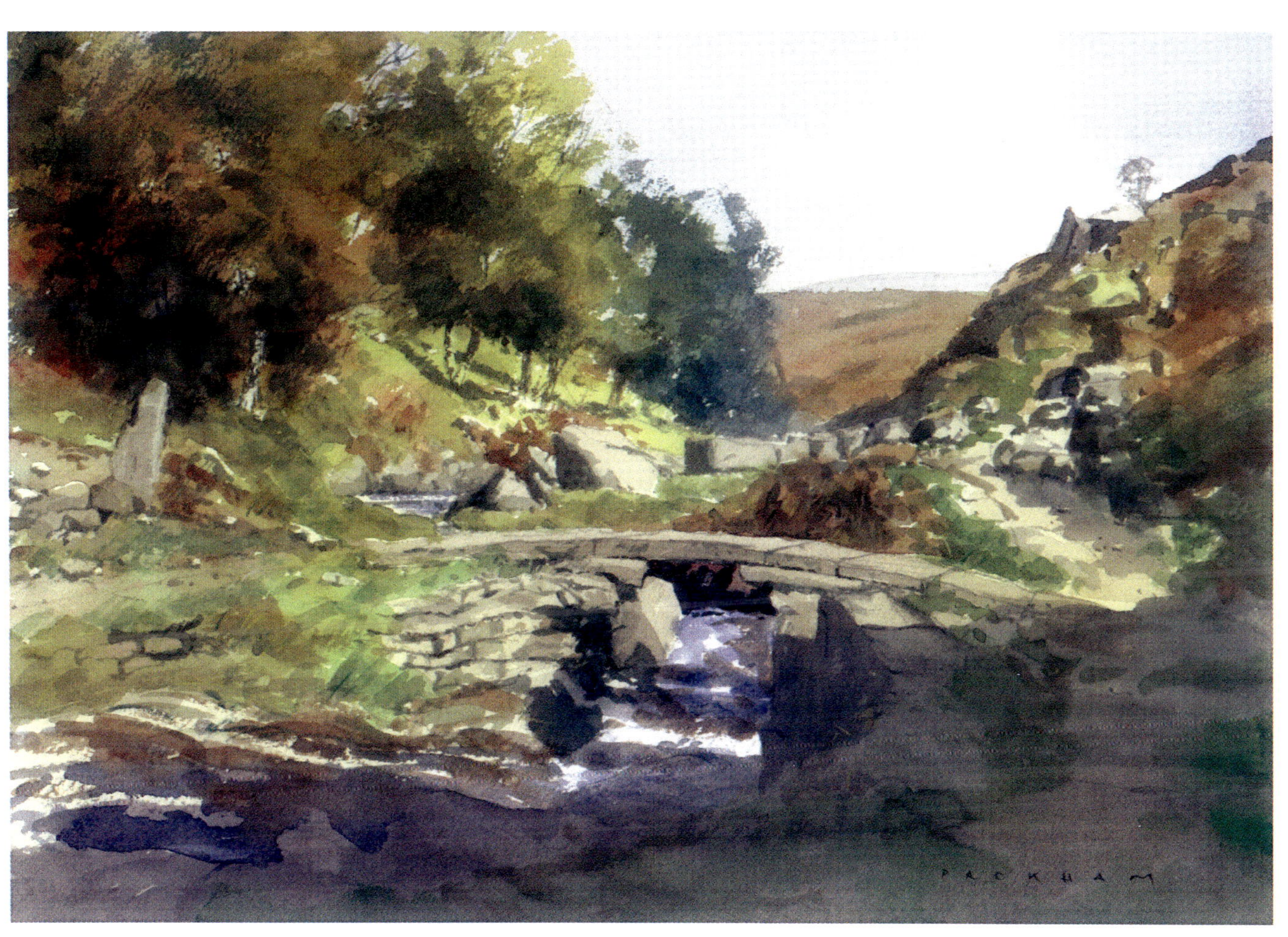
PACKHAM

LEVISHAM

LEVISHAM STATION AND its level crossing on the preserved North Yorkshire Moors railway make for an interesting composition. The station is more than a mile from the village, most of it up a very steep hill. Levisham is a favourite for walkers visiting the area and artists too.

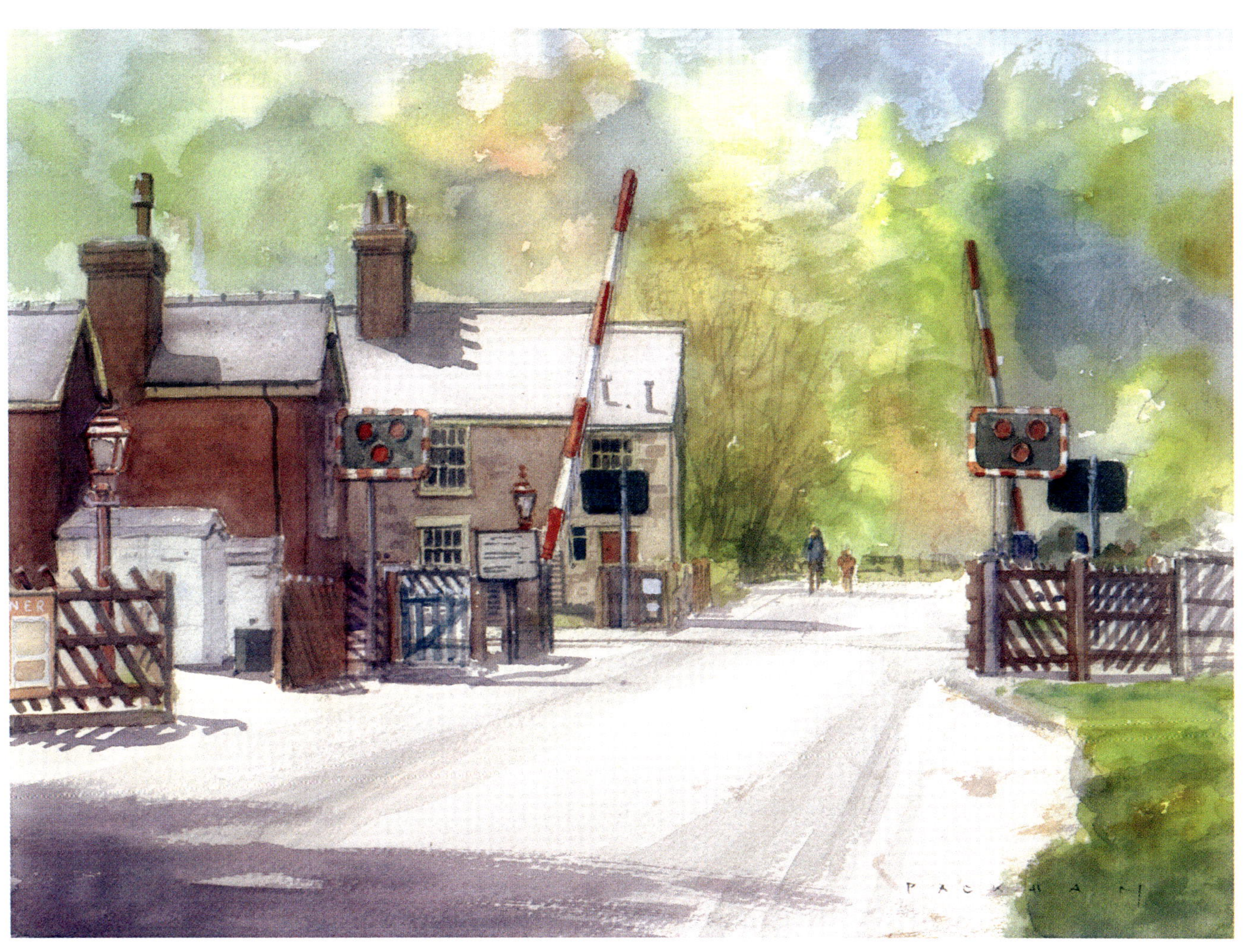
PACKHAM

STAITHES

ANOTHER STUDY OF a fishing boat in Staithes beck bottom, this time at low tide.

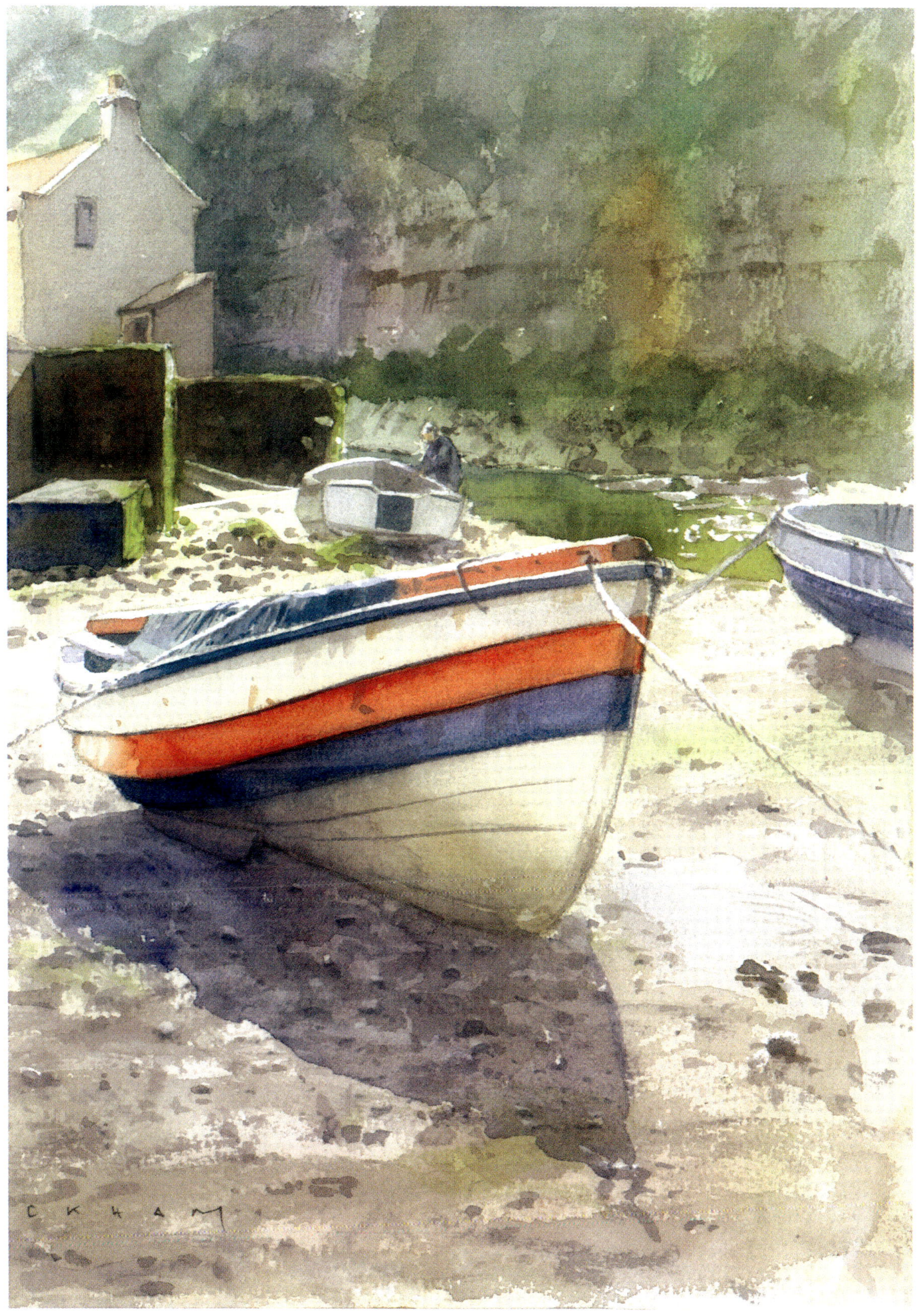

MIDDLESMOOR 1

THIS IS ONE of two studies of this attractive stone built village at the head of Nidderdale.

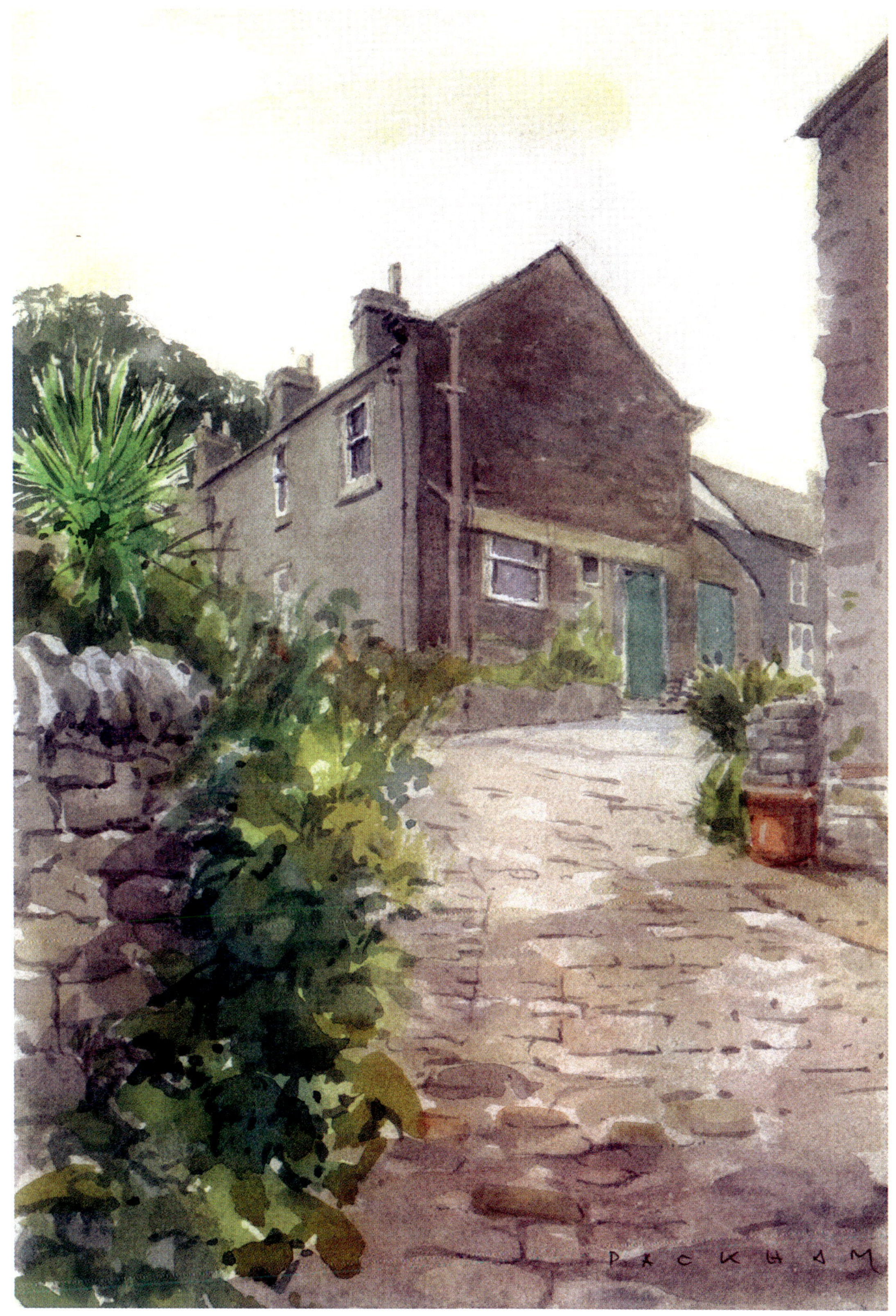
PACKHAM

MIDDLESMOOR 2

THIS IS THE other!

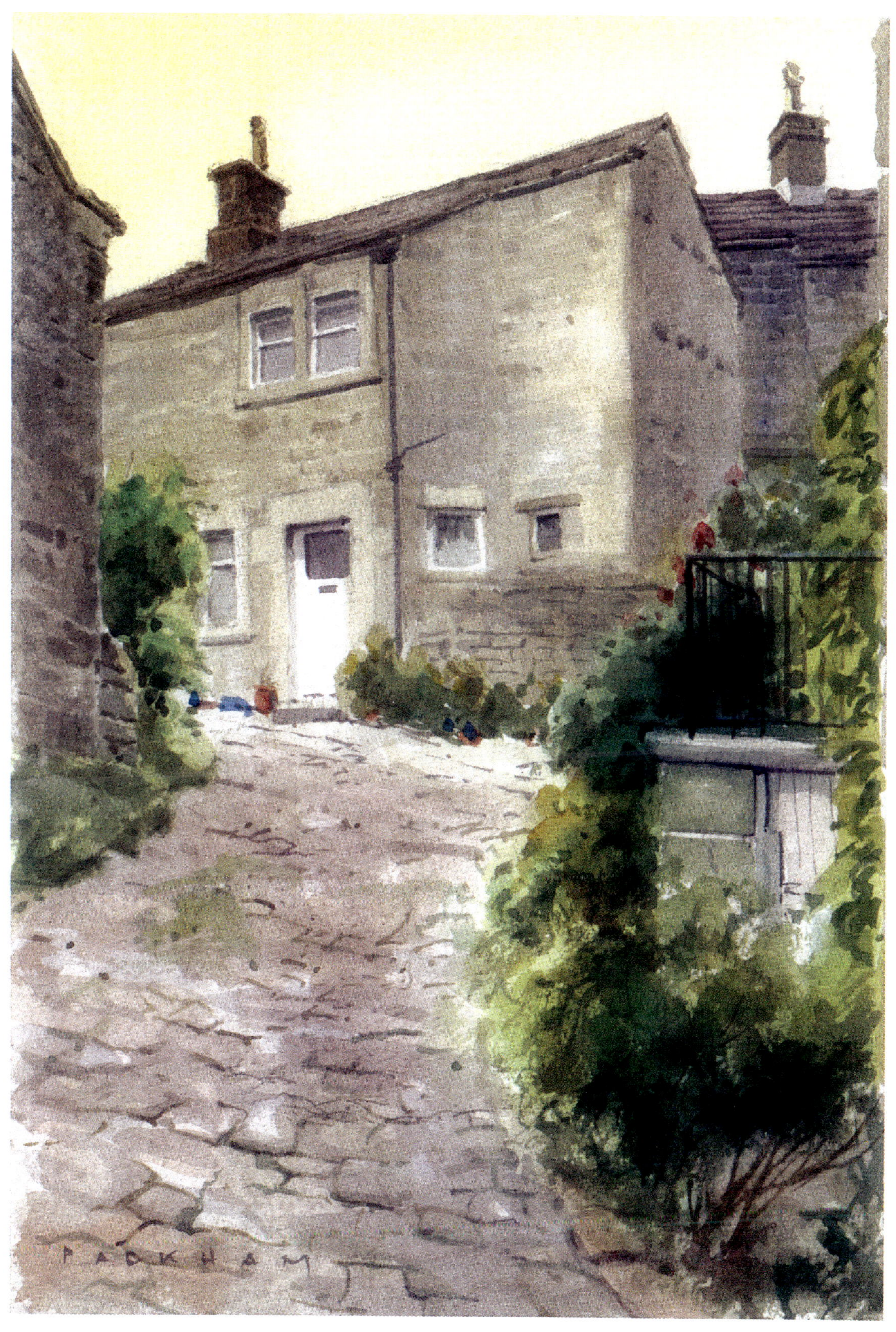
PACKHAM

NEWBIGGIN

A HOT SUMMER'S day at this secluded village just off the main road which runs through Bishopdale from Leyburn.

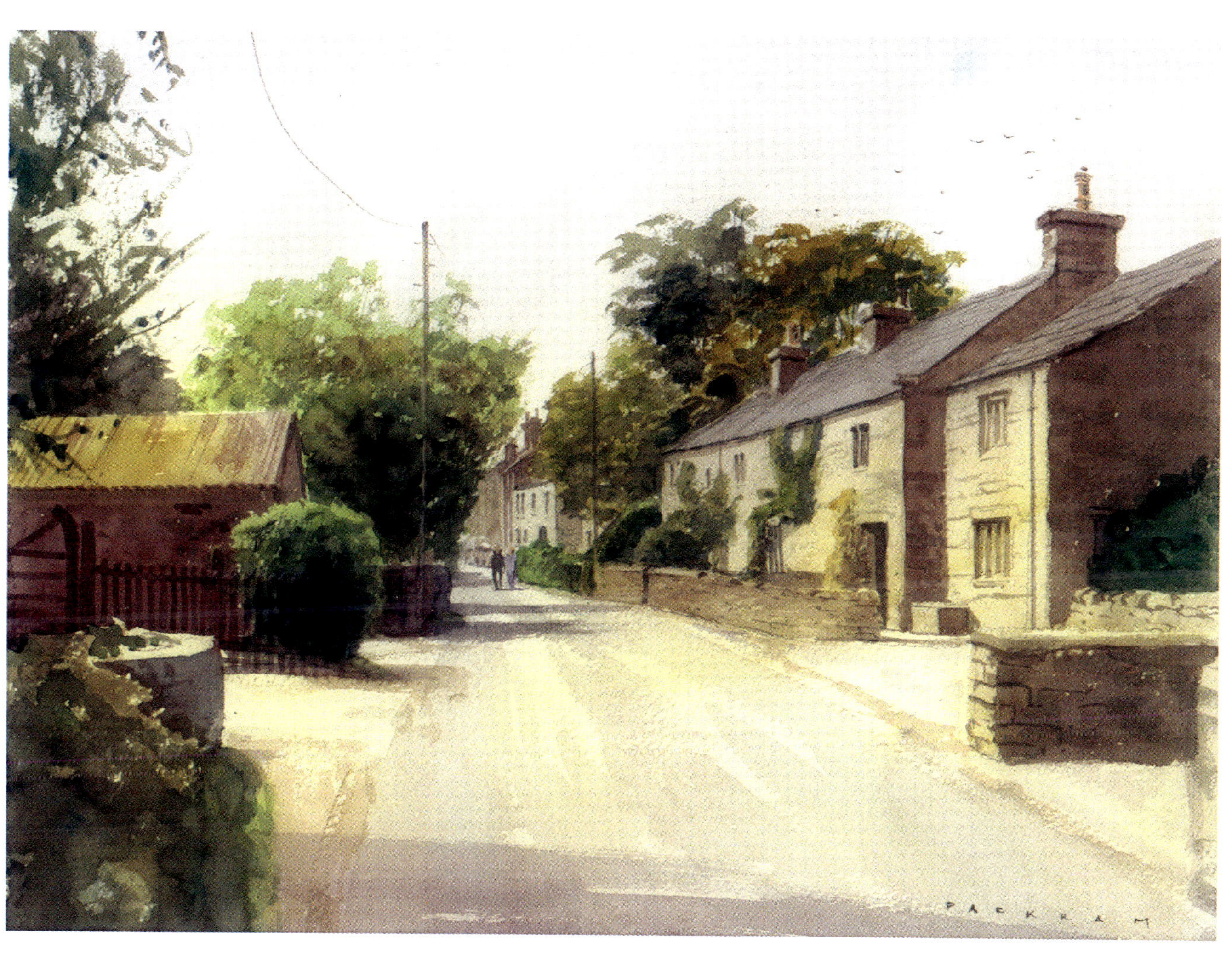
PACKHAM

SLAIDBURN

THIS LITTLE STUDY took my eye. It's on the river Hodder that runs through Slaidburn in the Trough of Bowland.

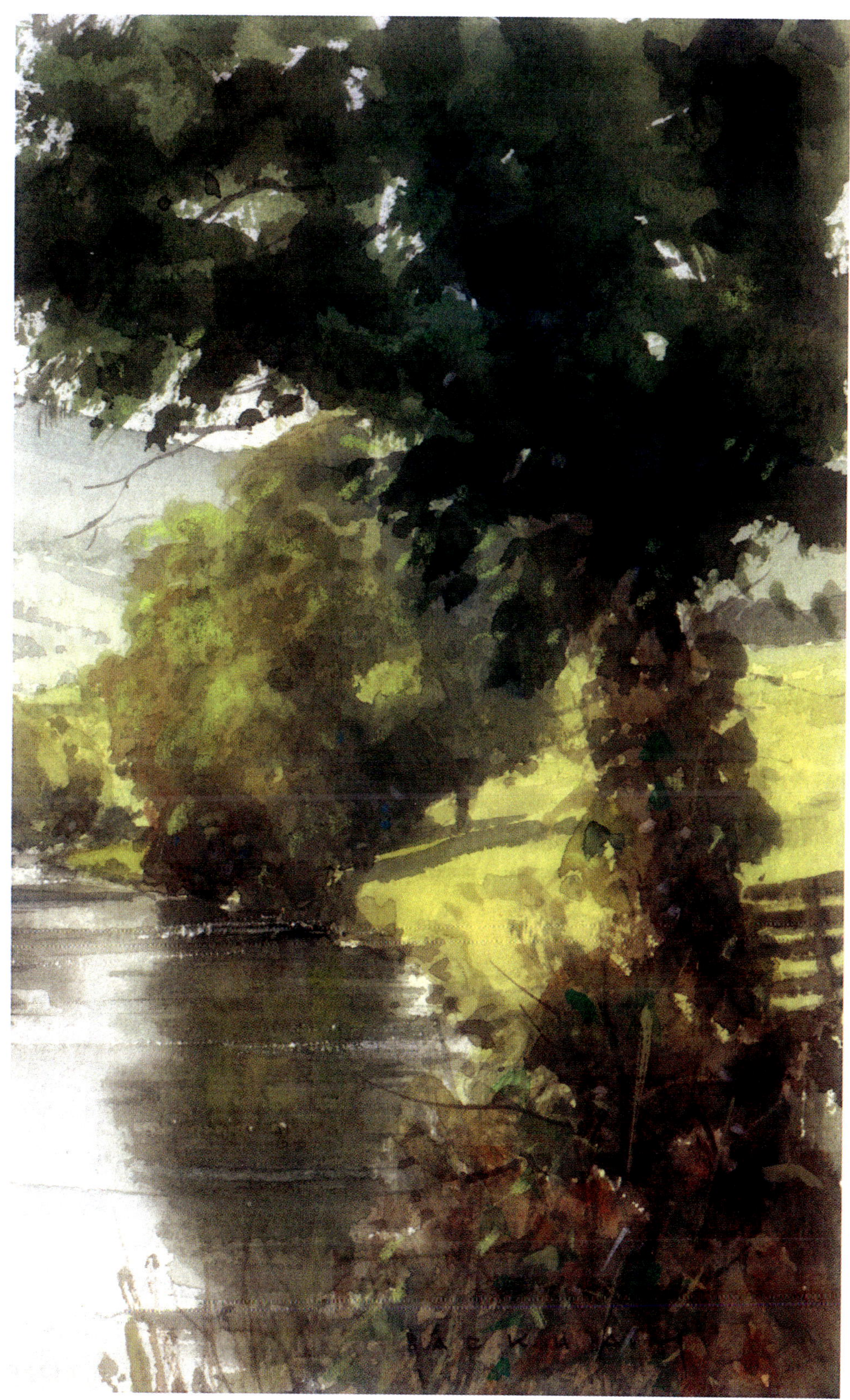

HEPTONSTALL

HEPTONSTALL CLINGS TO the hillside above the Calder Valley. Its main industry was home weaving and this can be seen in the character of the stone built houses which hasn't changed for centuries and, like many children before them, these young girls can play in the relative safety of these narrow cobbled streets.

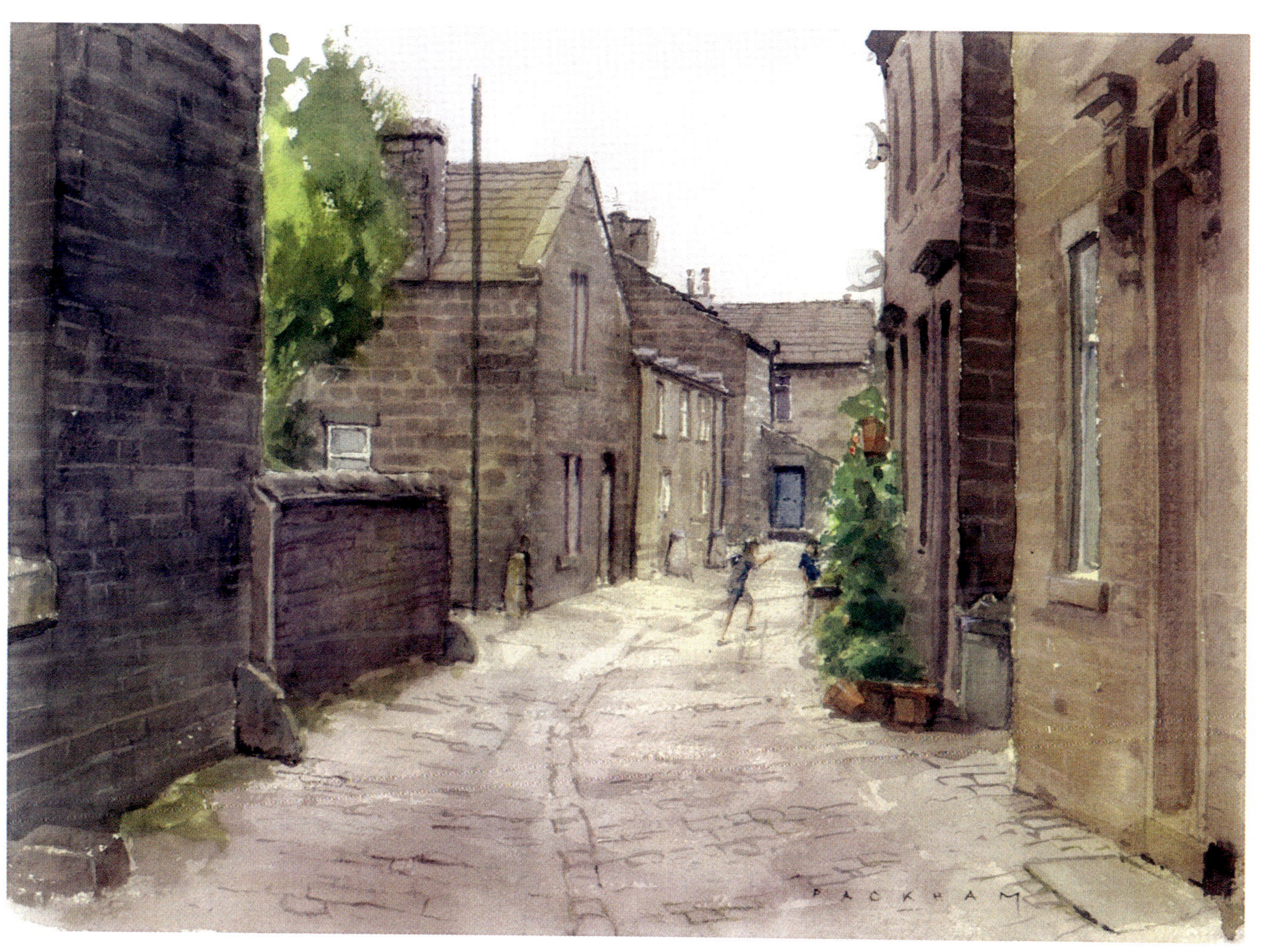
PACKHAM

HUDDERSFIELD

THIS INTERESTING FAÇADE in Huddersfield made a contrast to the modern car park opposite when I did the painting for an article in *Yorkshire ridings magazine*.

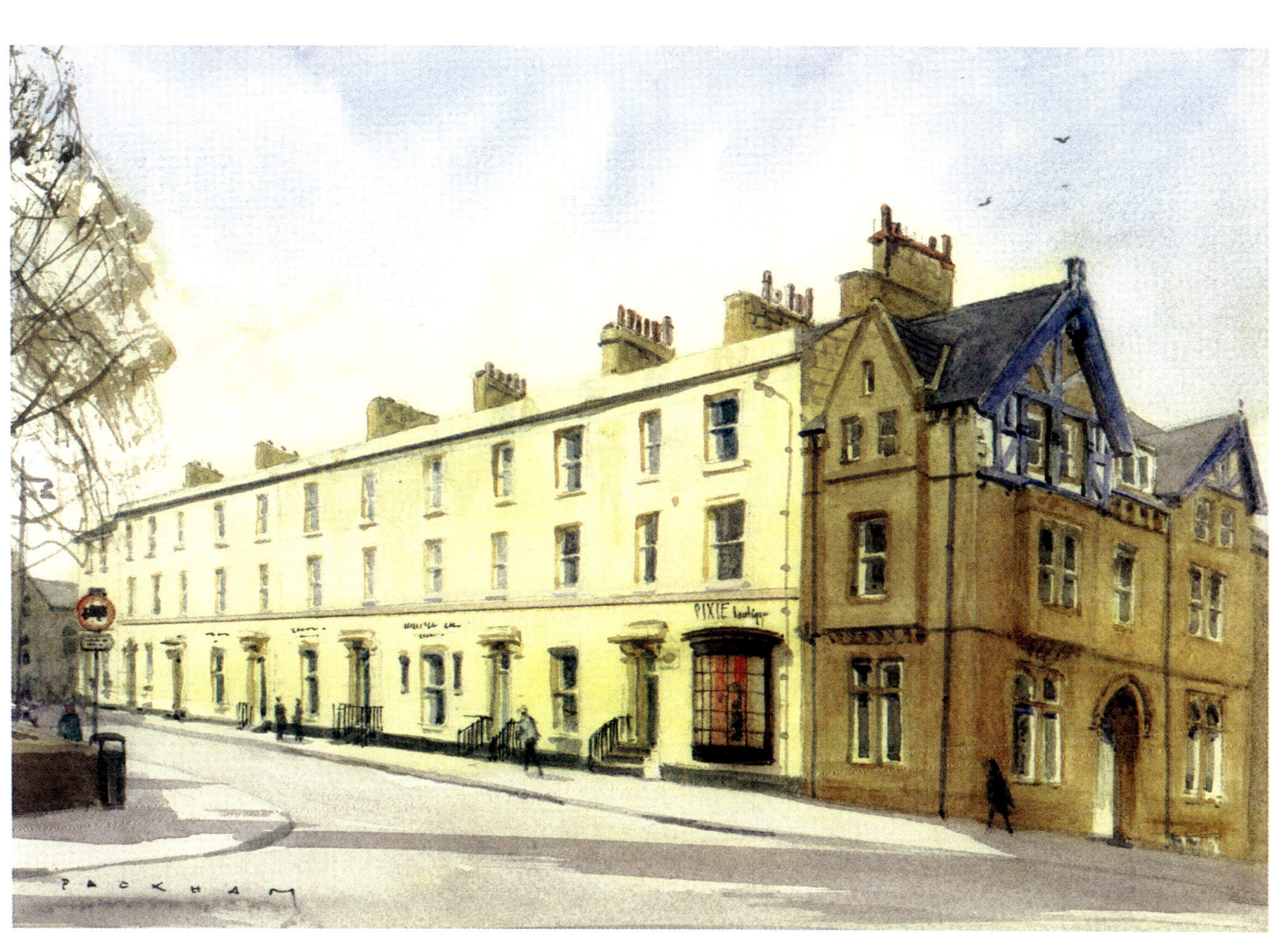
PIXIE
PACKHAM

BOSTON SPA

I HAVE ALWAYS enjoyed painting bridges and this handsome bridge over the river Wharfe at Boston Spa is a fine example. The angle I chose on this occasion was from the river bank looking back towards the bridge framed by the winter trees which I felt highlighted the architectural beauty of this fine structure.

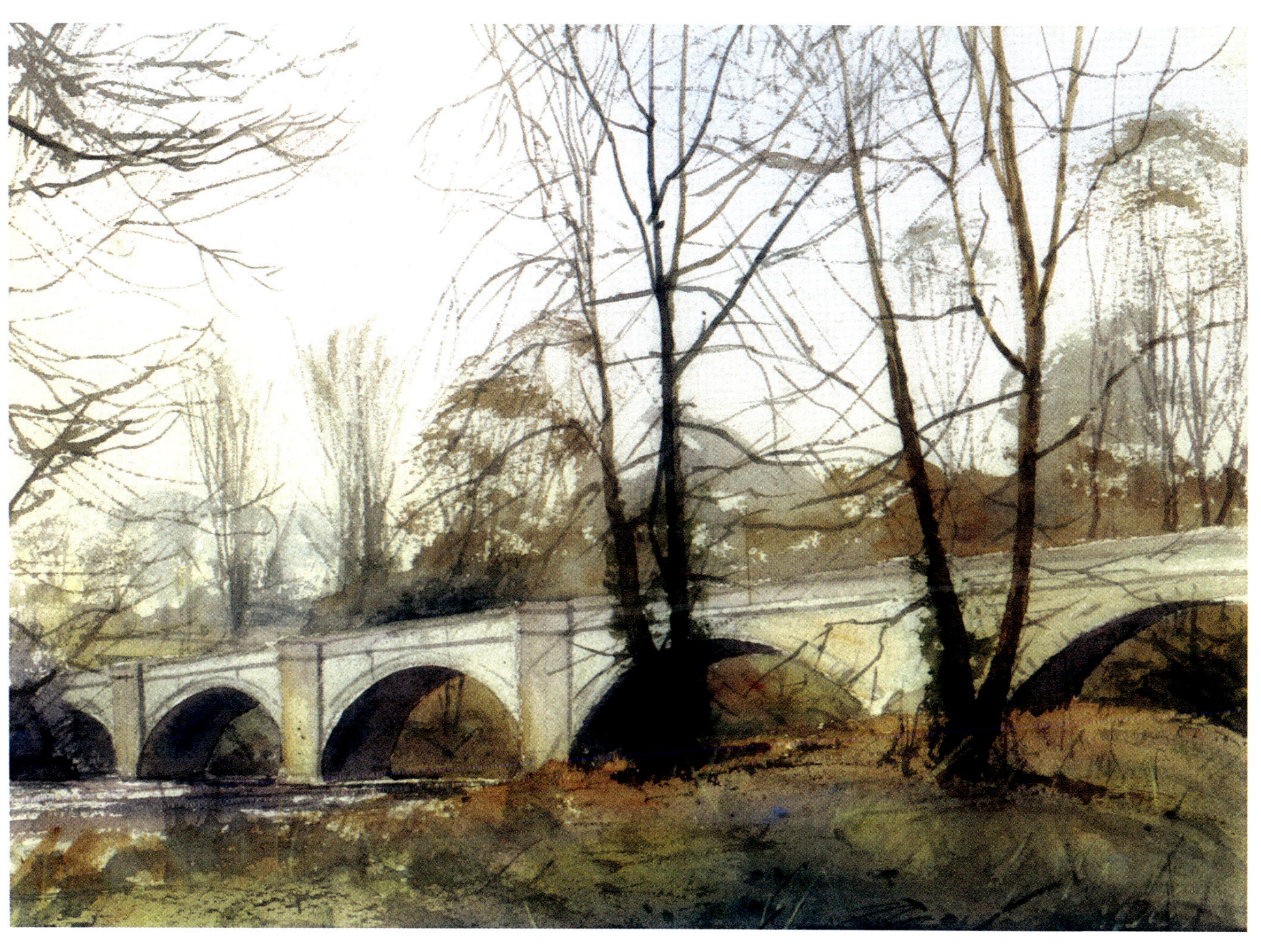

ILKLEY

I HAVE PAINTED the Cow and Calf rocks on Ilkley Moor on many occasions and from all angles but this unusual view I thought warranted a quick sketch on an early autumn afternoon.

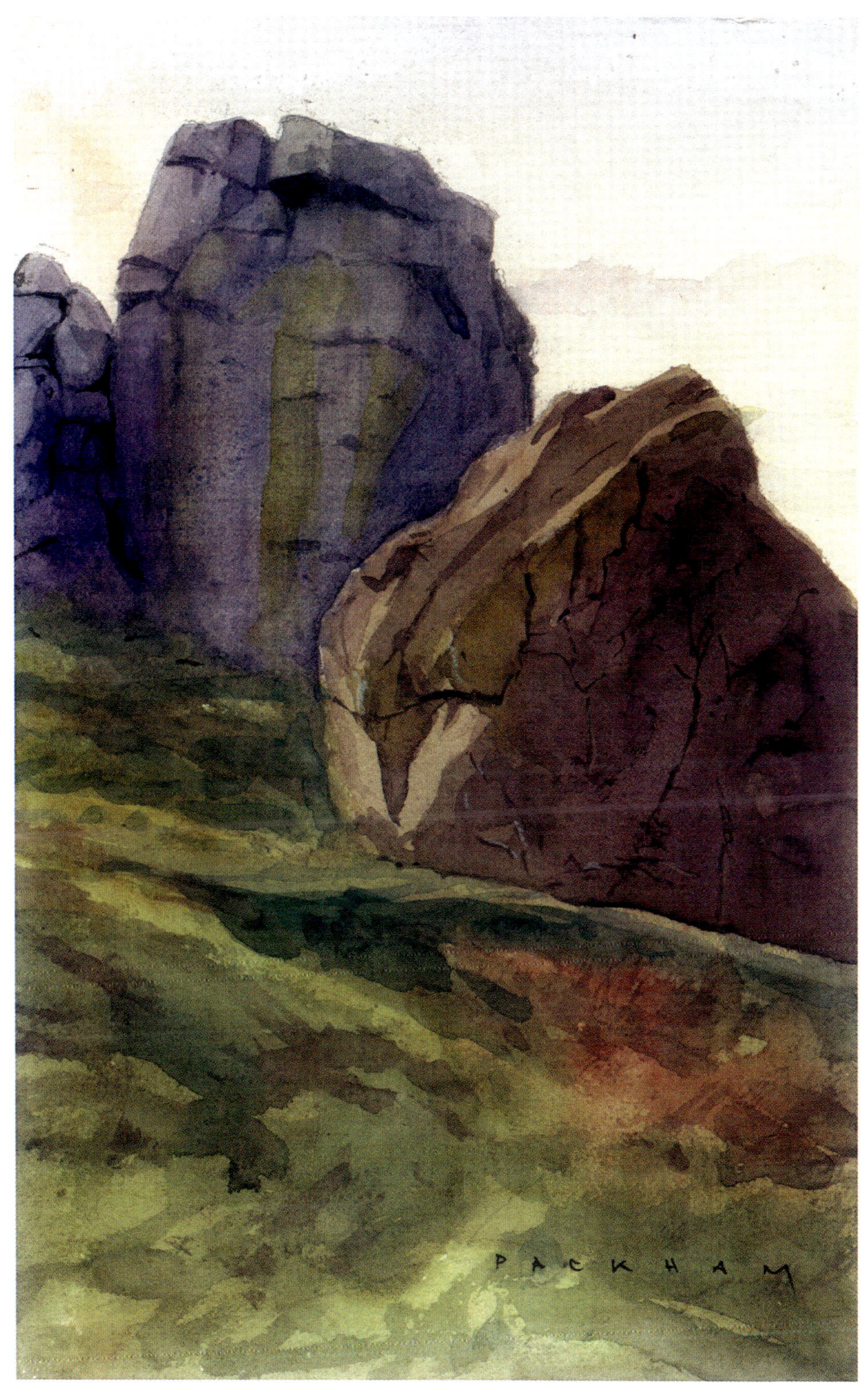
PACKHAM

BRIDLINGTON

THIS RED SAIL took my eye during a yacht race off the North Sea coast at Bridlington.

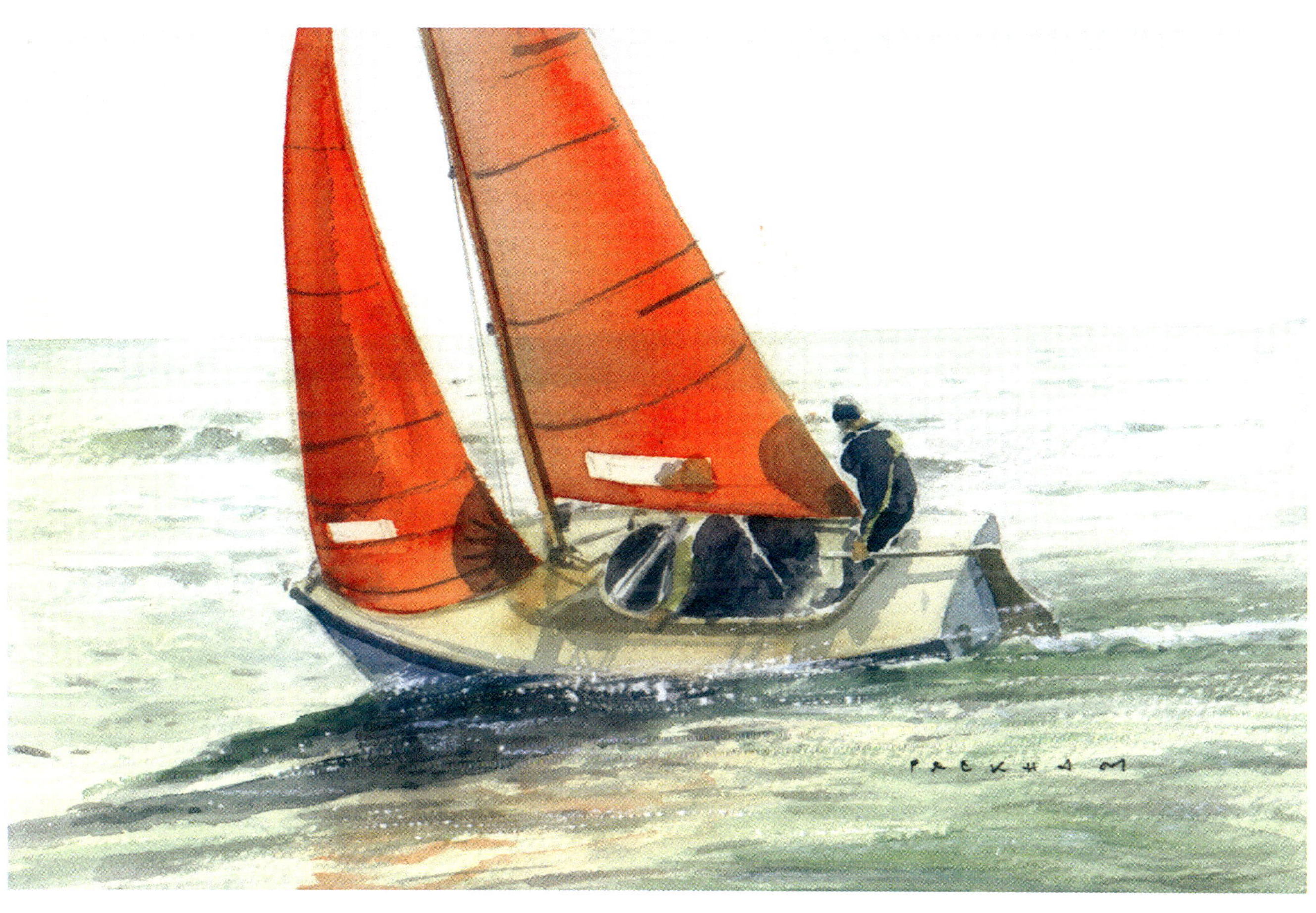
PECKHAM

BURNSALL

JUST UP STREAM from Burnsall is Loup Scar, the location from where Grassington blacksmith Tom Lee pushed the body of Dr Petty, whom he had previously murdered, in an effort to make it appear to be an accident. He was thwarted by a courting couple who had witnessed the whole incident which ultimately sent him to the gallows. It is a very beautiful section of the river Wharfe and part of a very attractive riverside walk.

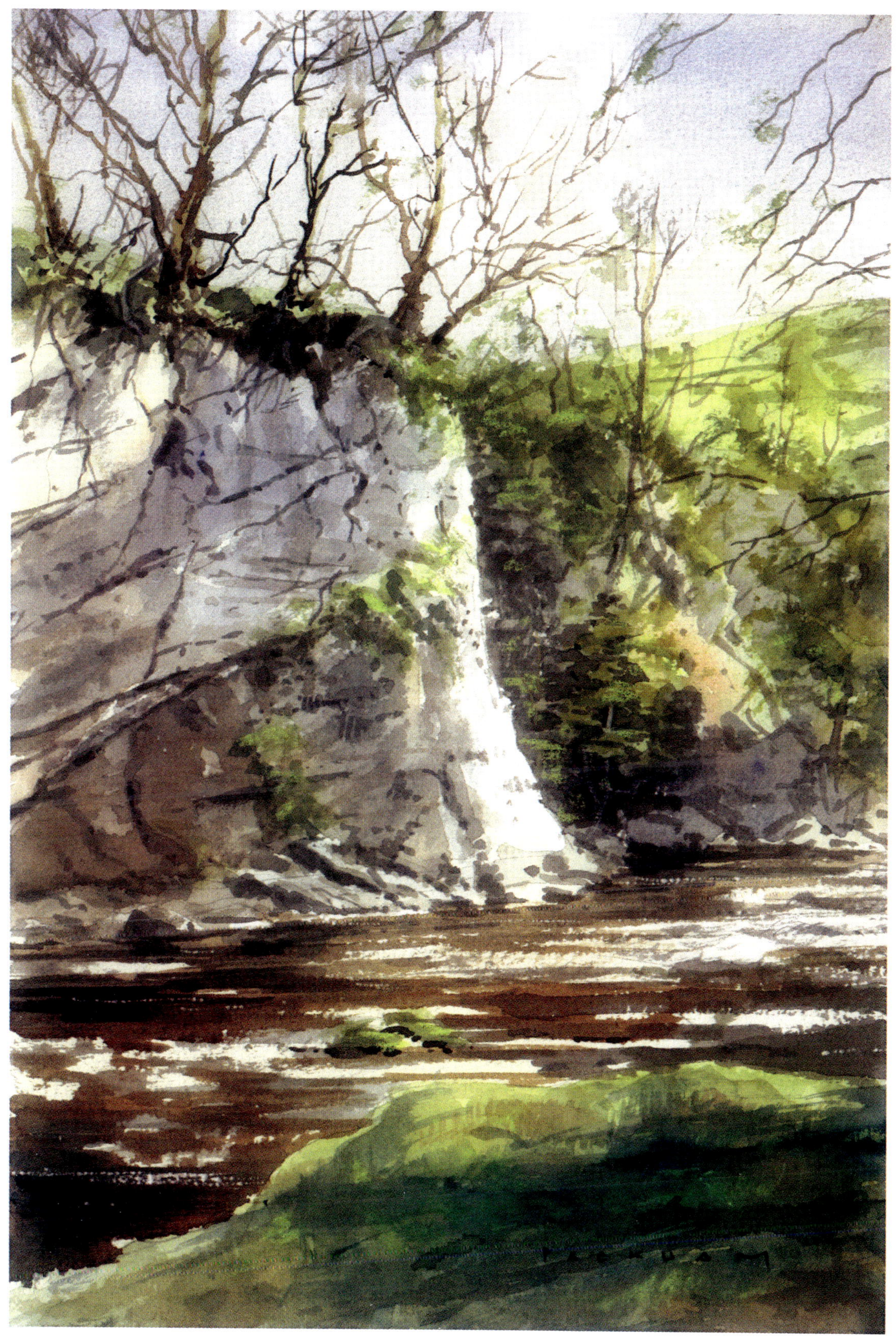

HEBDEN

THERE IS SOMETHING about fresh, crisp snow that I find particularly appealing, almost as if you are the first and only person to set foot in the area. It was just so when I came across this lone sheep on the old miners' bridge which straddles Hebden Ghyll and I felt it made a perfect composition in wintry conditions.

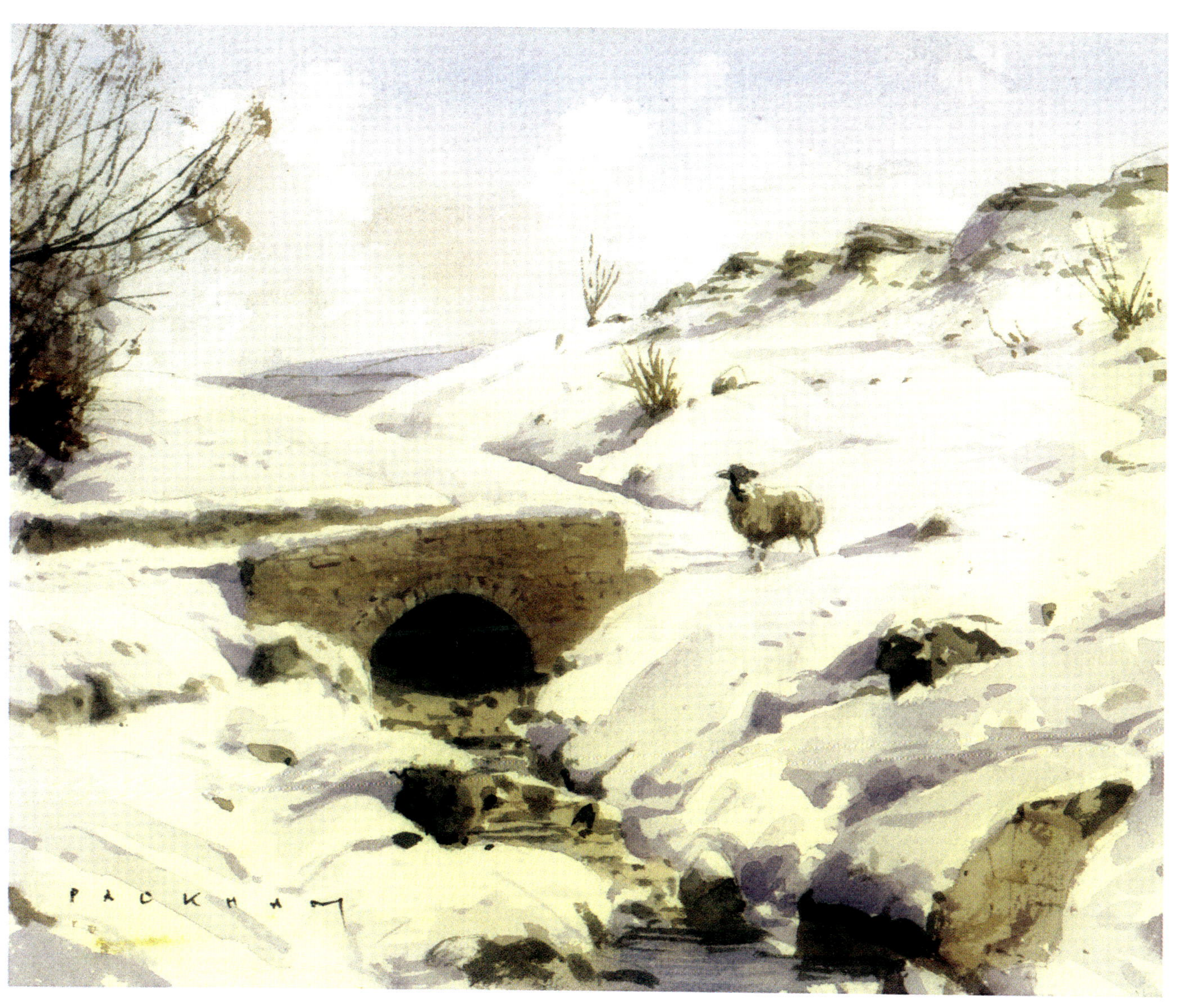
PACKHAM

SHEFFIELD

OVER THE PAST few years I have become more and more attracted to painting woodland – especially in winter. Sheffield is surrounded by some of the county's finest woodland and this, coupled with the harsh winter of 2009/10, inspired me to paint this scene in Wharncliffe Woods near to the village of Grenoside.

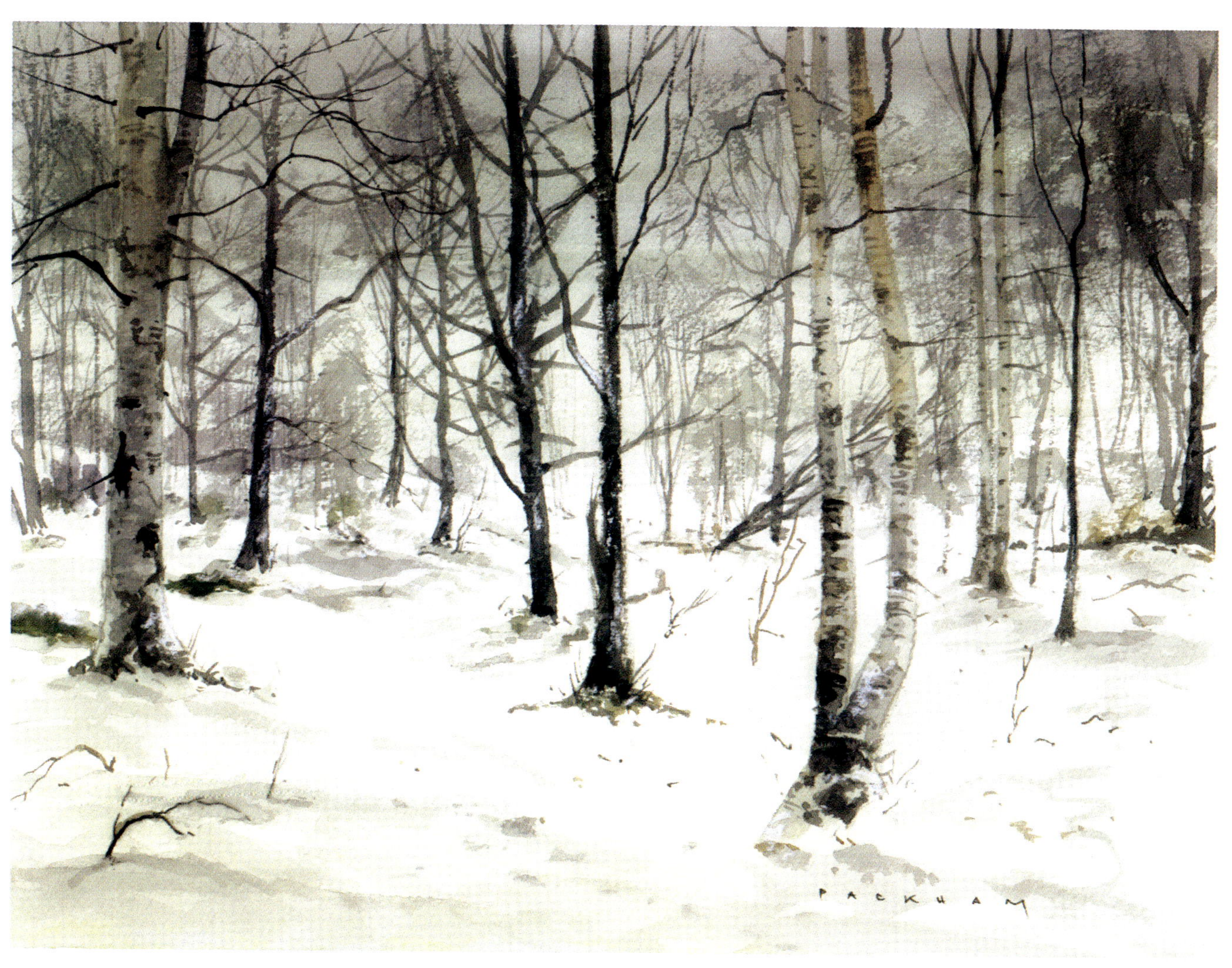
PACKHAM

SOUTH DALTON

THE GENTLE YORKSHIRE Wolds are probably the least painted area of Yorkshire but I find they have a wonderful charm of their own and certainly warrant being captured in a painting. South Dalton is typical of the attractive villages to be found there.

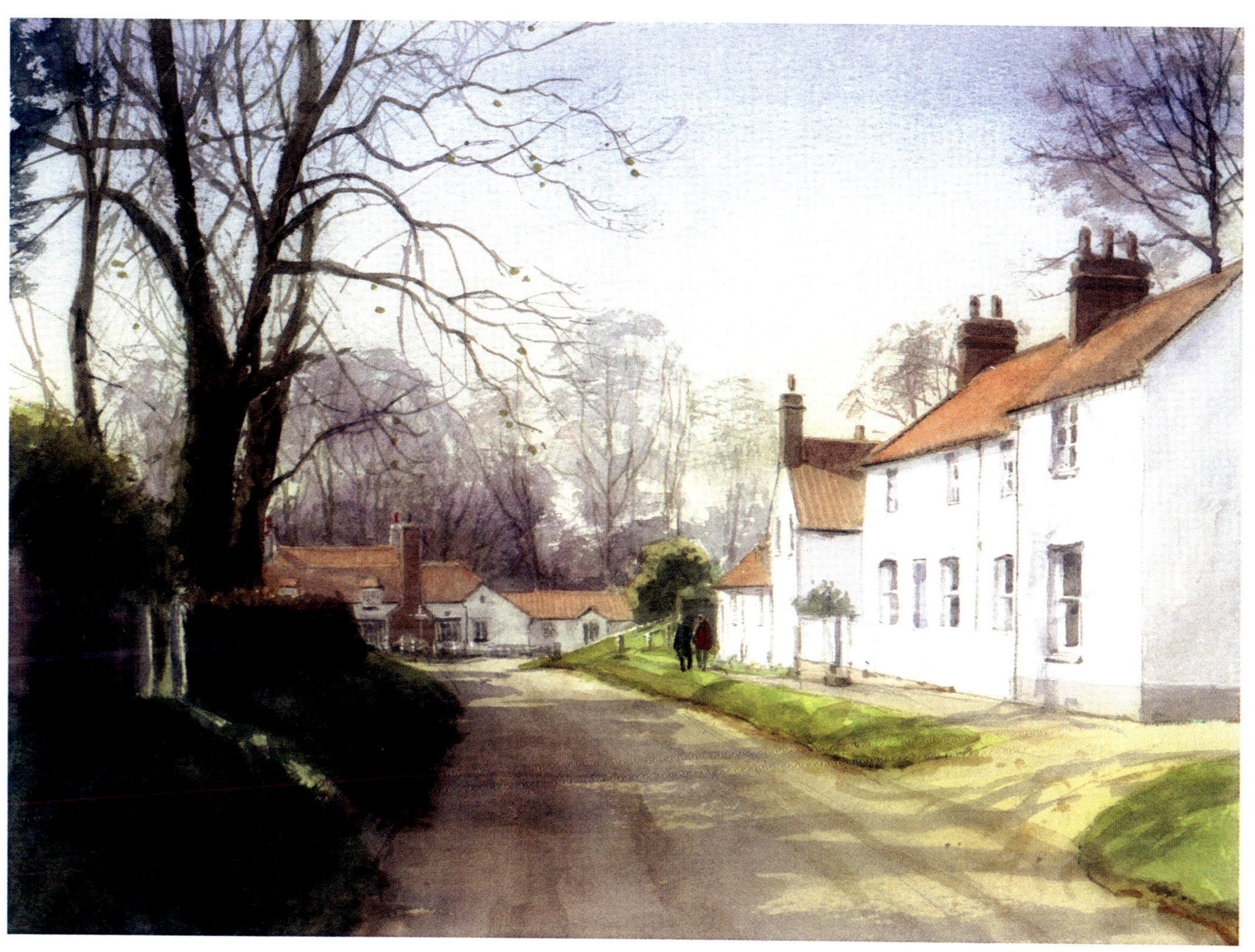

THORPE IN THE HOLLOW

ONE OF THE hidden gems of Wharfedale – Thorpe can be found just off the Wharfedale road between Burnsall and Threshfield. Legend has it that many years ago when the Scots raided this part of the Dales on their journey south Thorpe remained totally undiscovered and unscathed and it is not hard to see why.

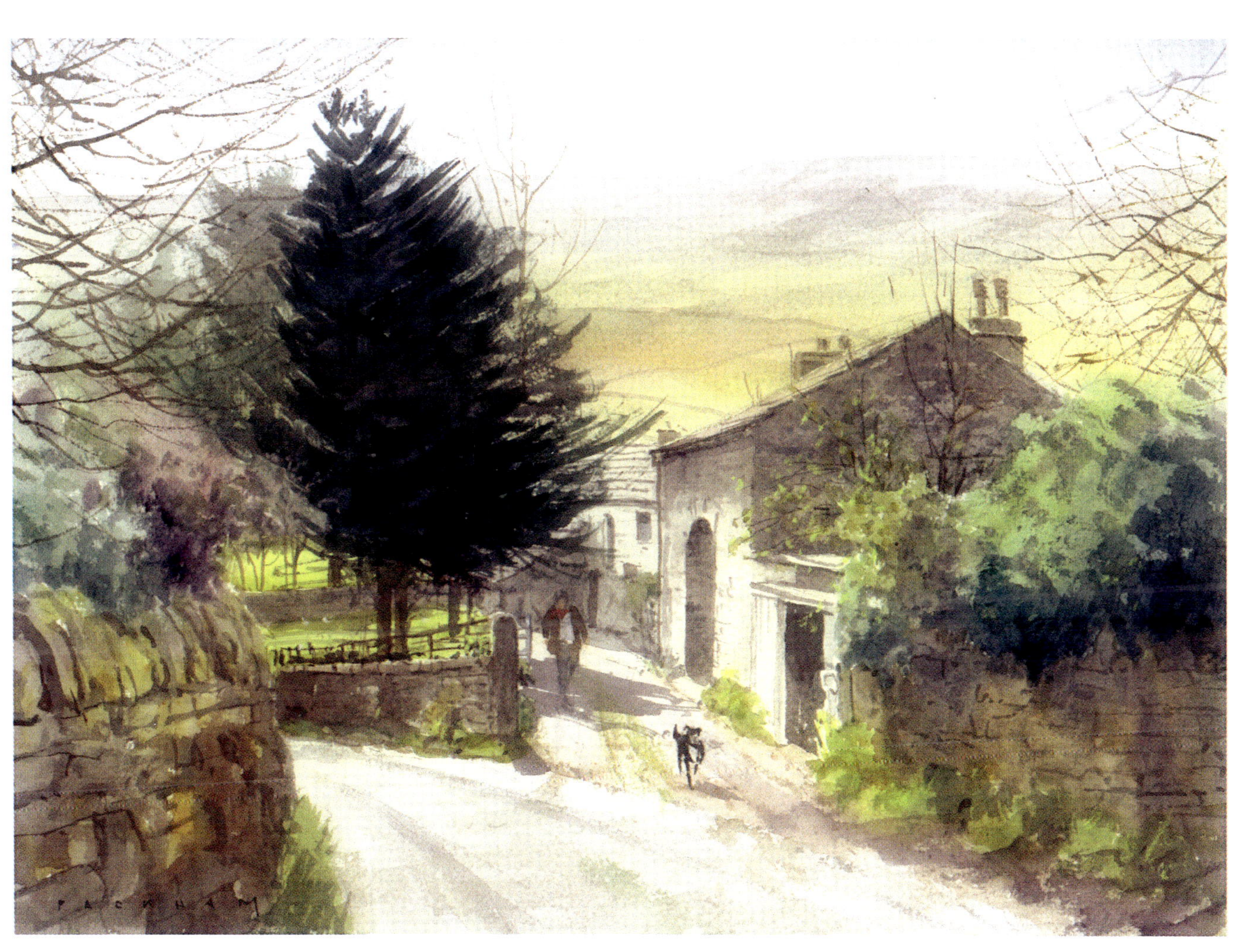
PACKHAM

HARDCASTLE CRAGGS

THIS WONDERFUL WOODED valley near Hebden Bridge is so tranquil it seems hard to believe that Gibson Mill together with a few cottages would be built here. It was built as a cotton mill in 1800 but it was later in the 1900s it was transformed into a place of entertainment for the local people and included a dance hall, roller skating rink and boating on the lake. The site is now under the careful ownership of the National Trust.

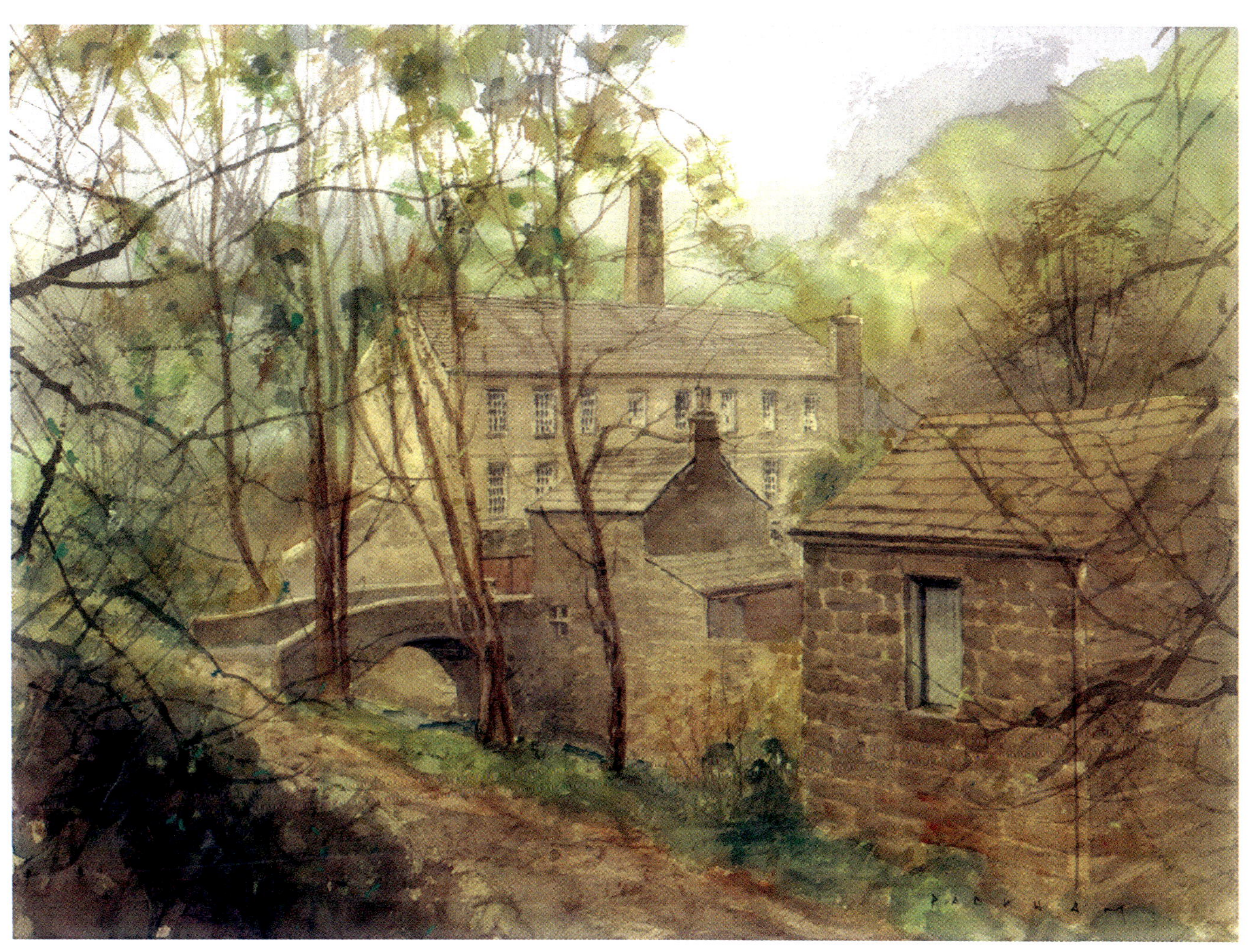
PACKHAM

STALLING BUSK

STALLING BUSK IS one of three small settlements based around the beautiful area of Semerwater and lies just south of the lake. This is a most attractive and unspoiled area and the cottages I have painted have a wonderful feeling of tranquillity. It makes one want to linger a while and enjoy the peace and quiet.

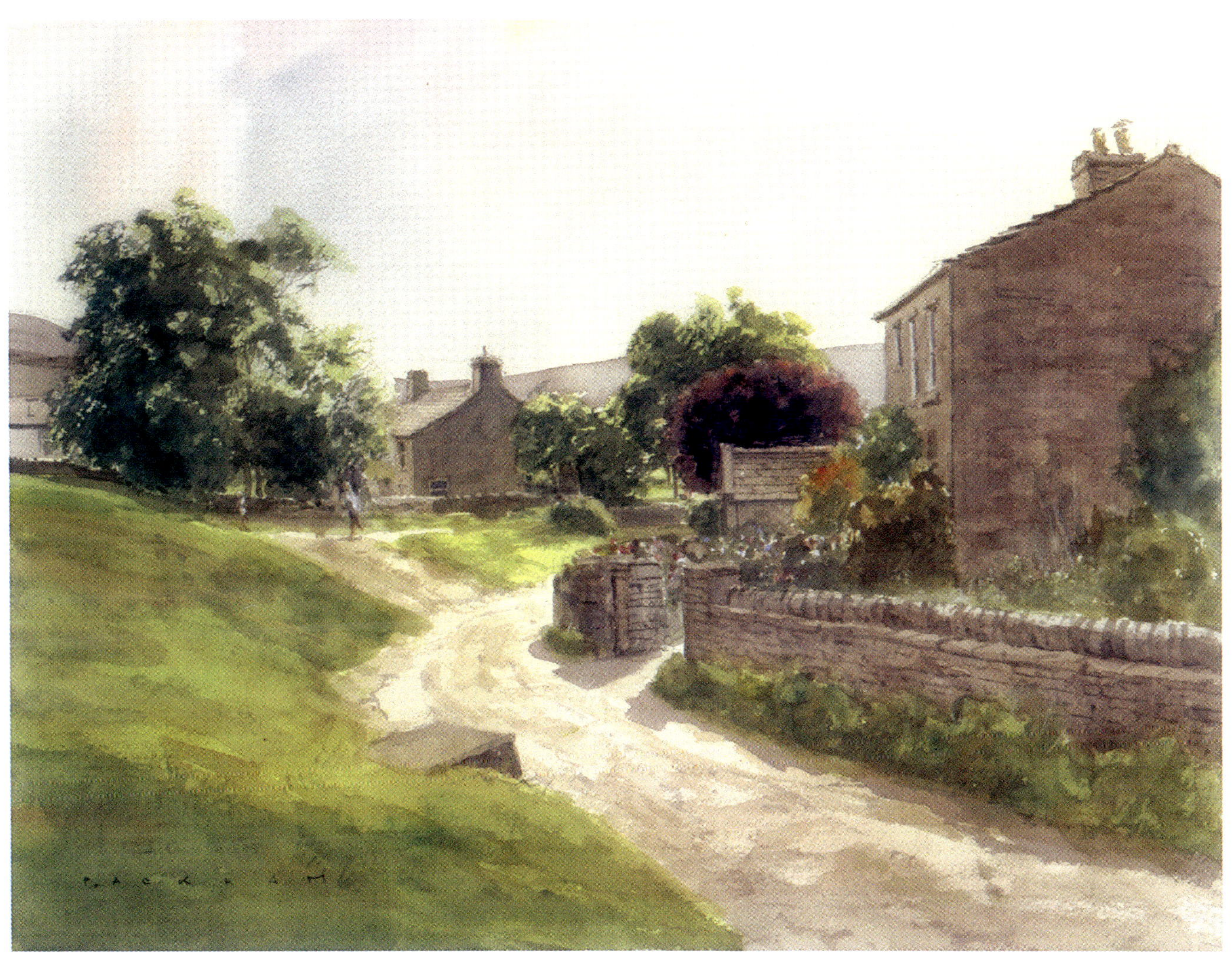
PACKHAM

WHITBY

ONE OF THE most painted coastal areas, Whitby can provide the artist with a view from almost any angle. However, this distant view is from the Scarborough road with a storm approaching and with Hawsker Church prominent in the middle distance.

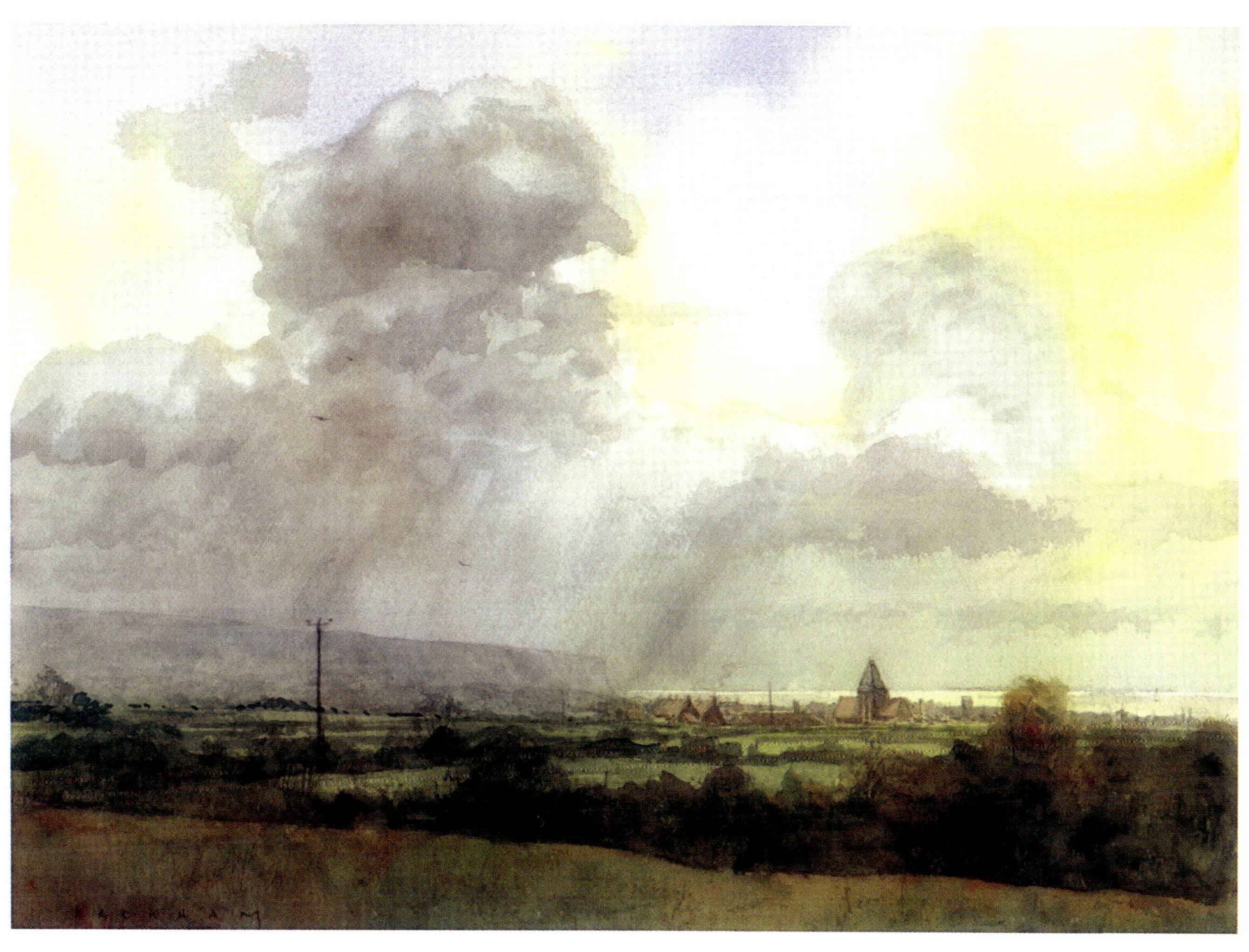

MARSDEN

I FOUND THIS particular subject of Tenter Posts in the locality of Marsden. History has it that they had hooks attached and were used for the stretching and drying of new cloth.

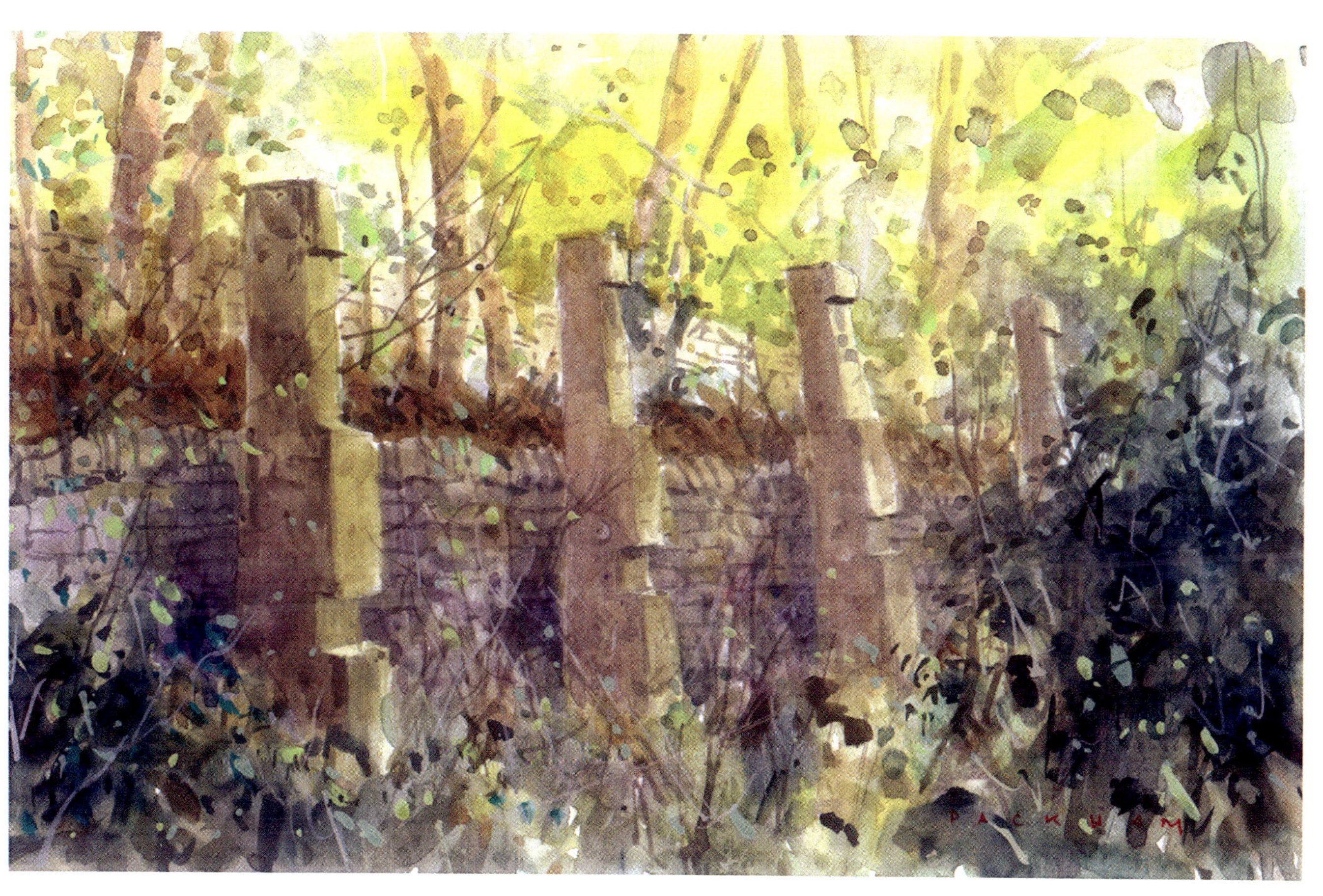
PACKHAM

APPLETREEWICK

THIS IS PROBABLY the first view of Aptrick (dialect used for this area) when approaching from the south. Steeped with history this little village is set within the heart of Wharfedale and provides visitors with wonderful river walks and an abundance of natural beauty.

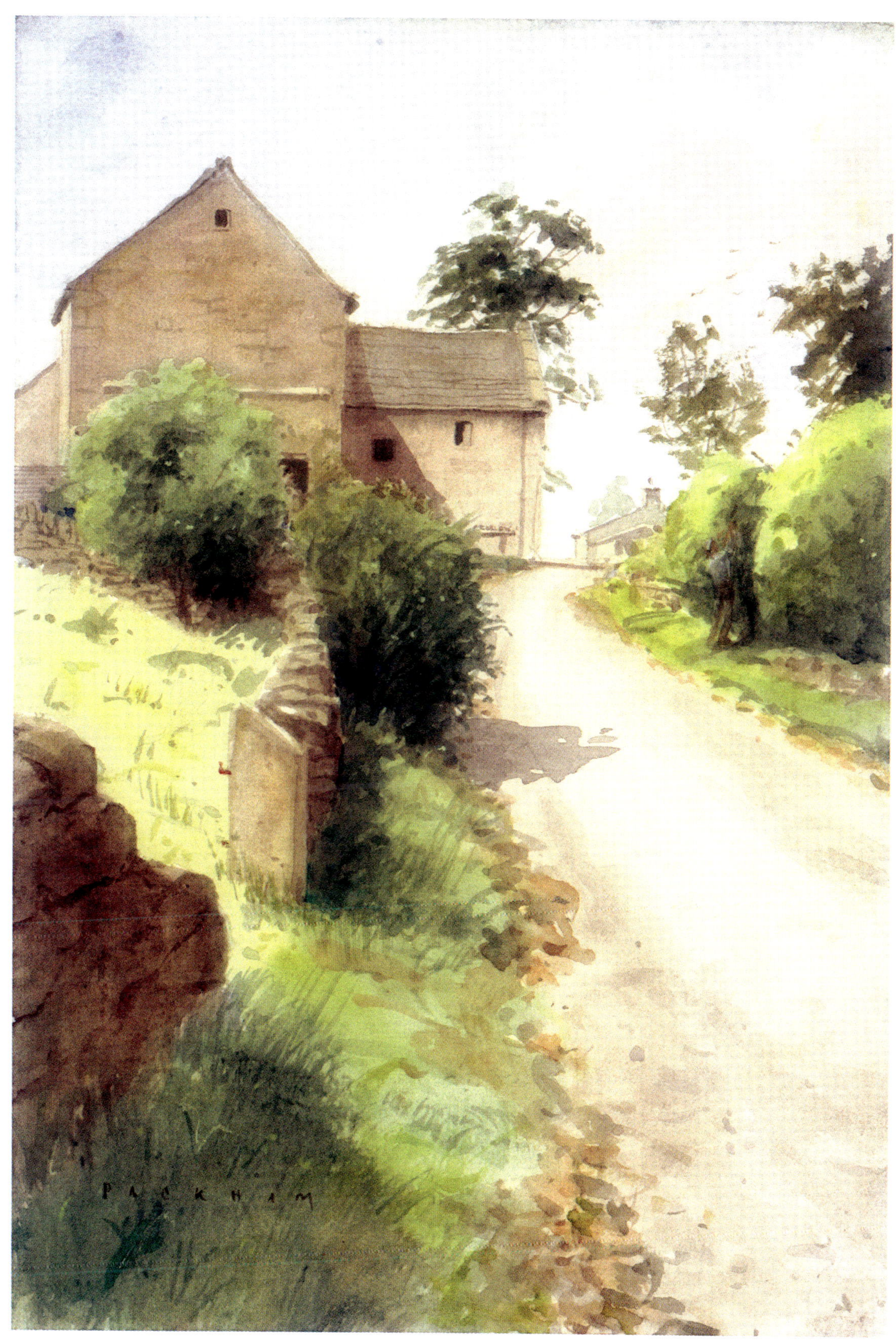
PACKHAM

THWAITE

I MAKE NO apology for including yet another view of this most interesting village. Swaledale is considered by many to be the most beautiful of the Yorkshire Dales. Most of the village dates back to the 18th and 19th centuries and literally provides a painting around every corner.

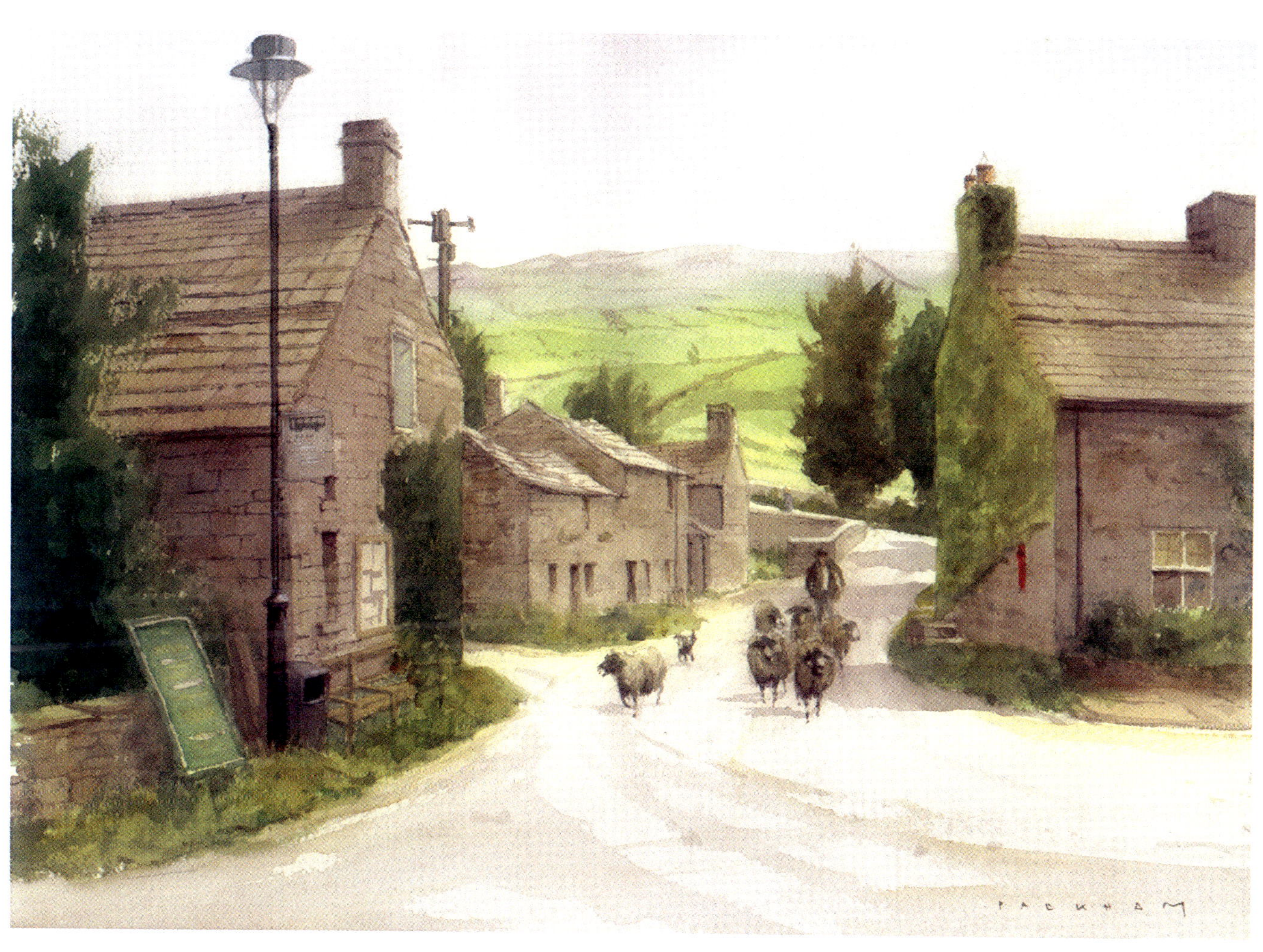

DOWNHOLME

IT SEEMS FOR some reason I have overlooked this very attractive area round Richmond. Doing my research for this book I came across this lovely area and immediately observed a picture just asking to be painted.

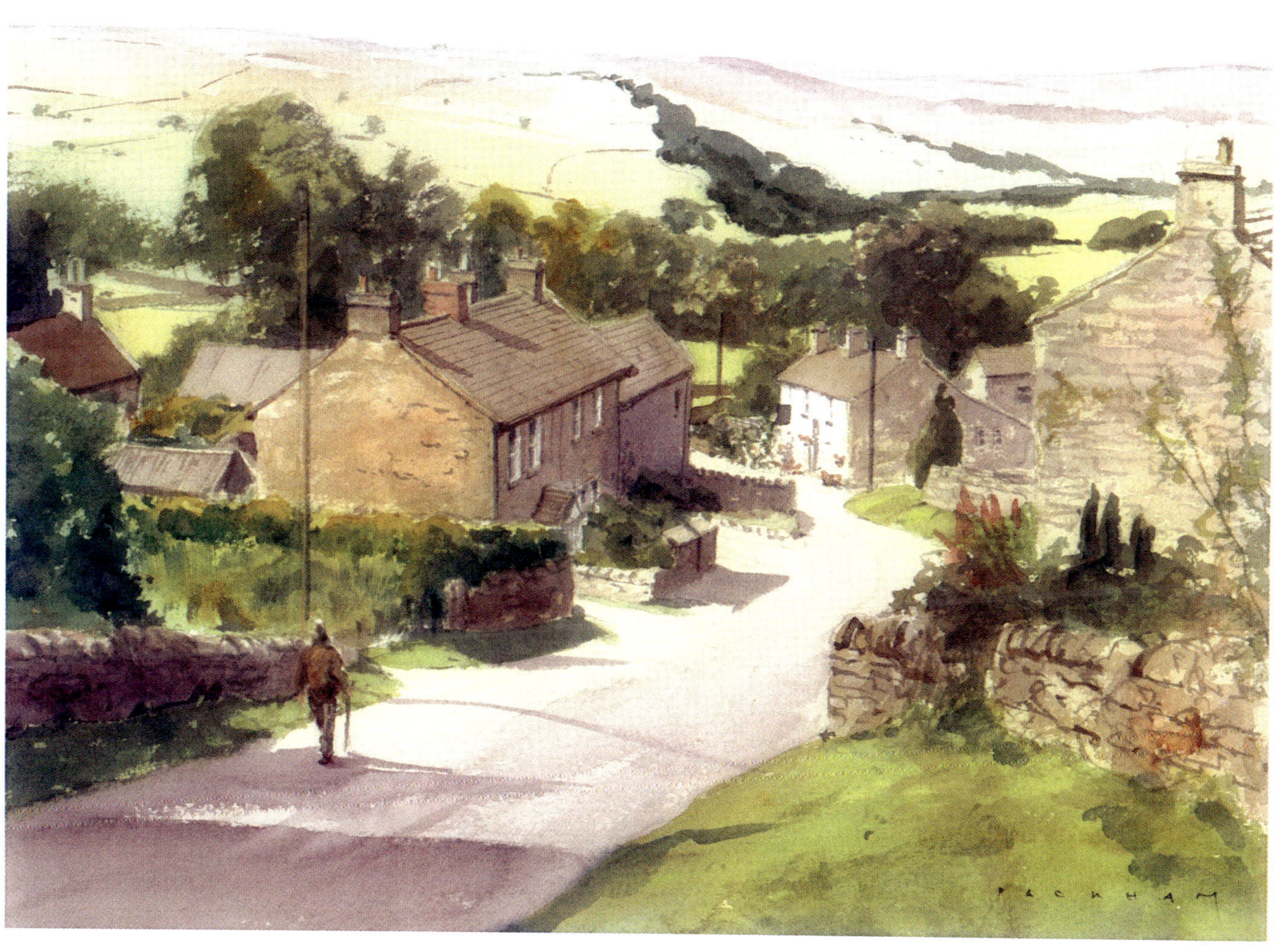
PECKHAM

HEPTONSTALL

THIS VIEW OF Whitehall farm in Heptonstall portrays the rugged atmosphere of this Pennine village which historically was a centre for handloom weaving and the site of a battle in 1643 during the English Civil War.

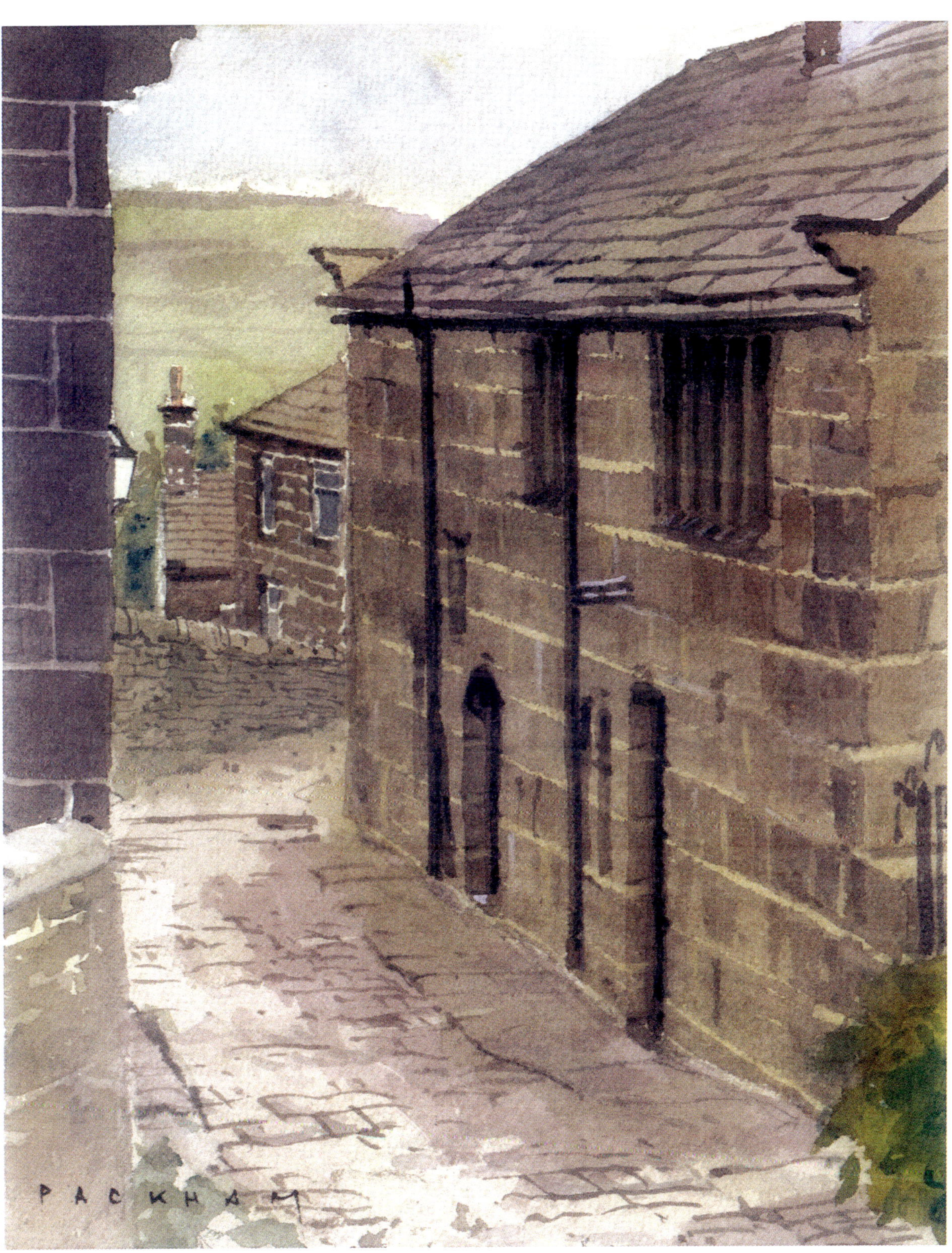
PACKHAM

APPLETREEWICK

THIS LATE WINTER view is from the southern end of the village looking south east past the Craven Arms towards Simon's Seat on Barden Fell.

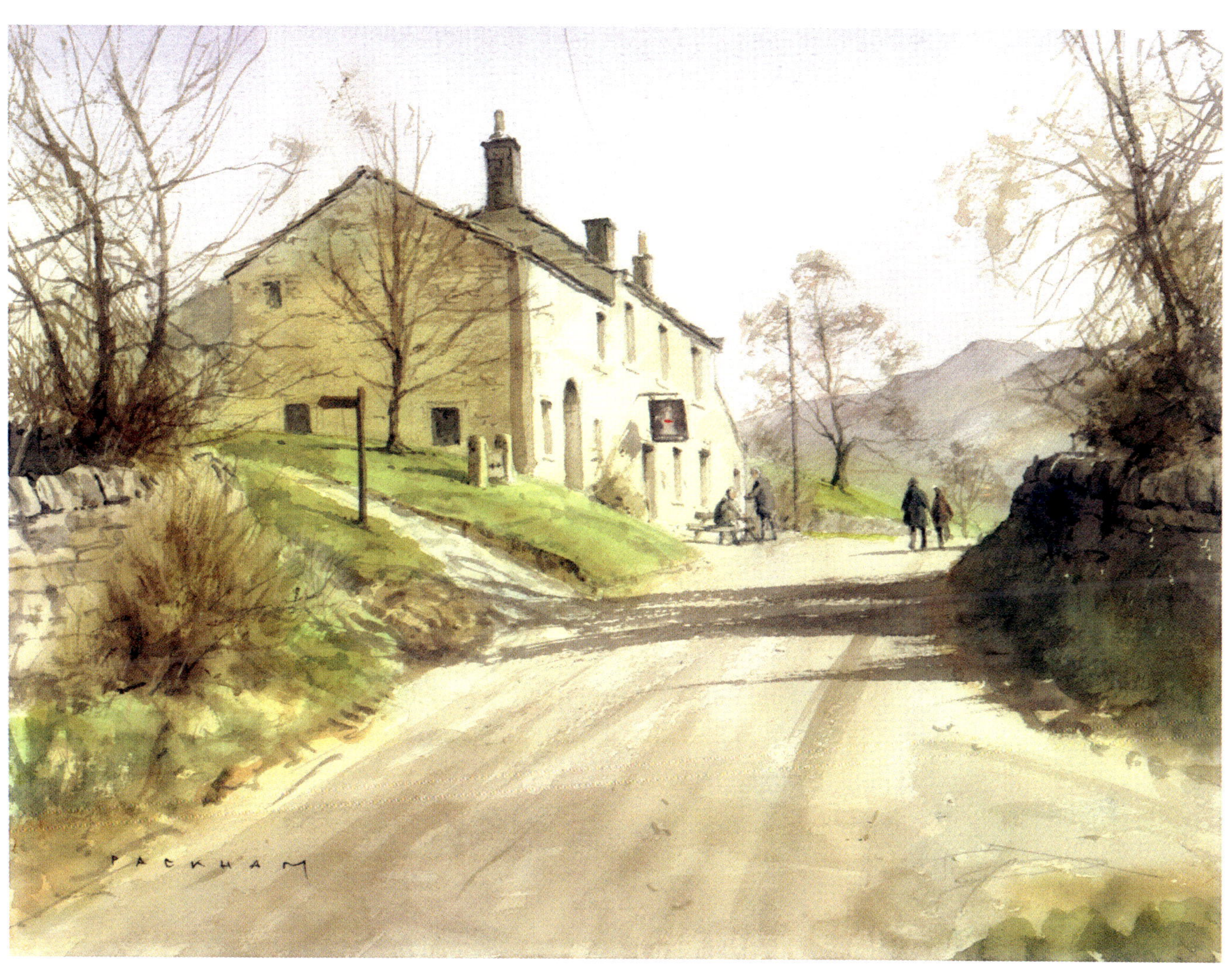
PACKHAM

DRIFFIELD

DRIFFIELD IS A market town in the East Riding of Yorkshire and provided this fine Wolds view in early autumn.

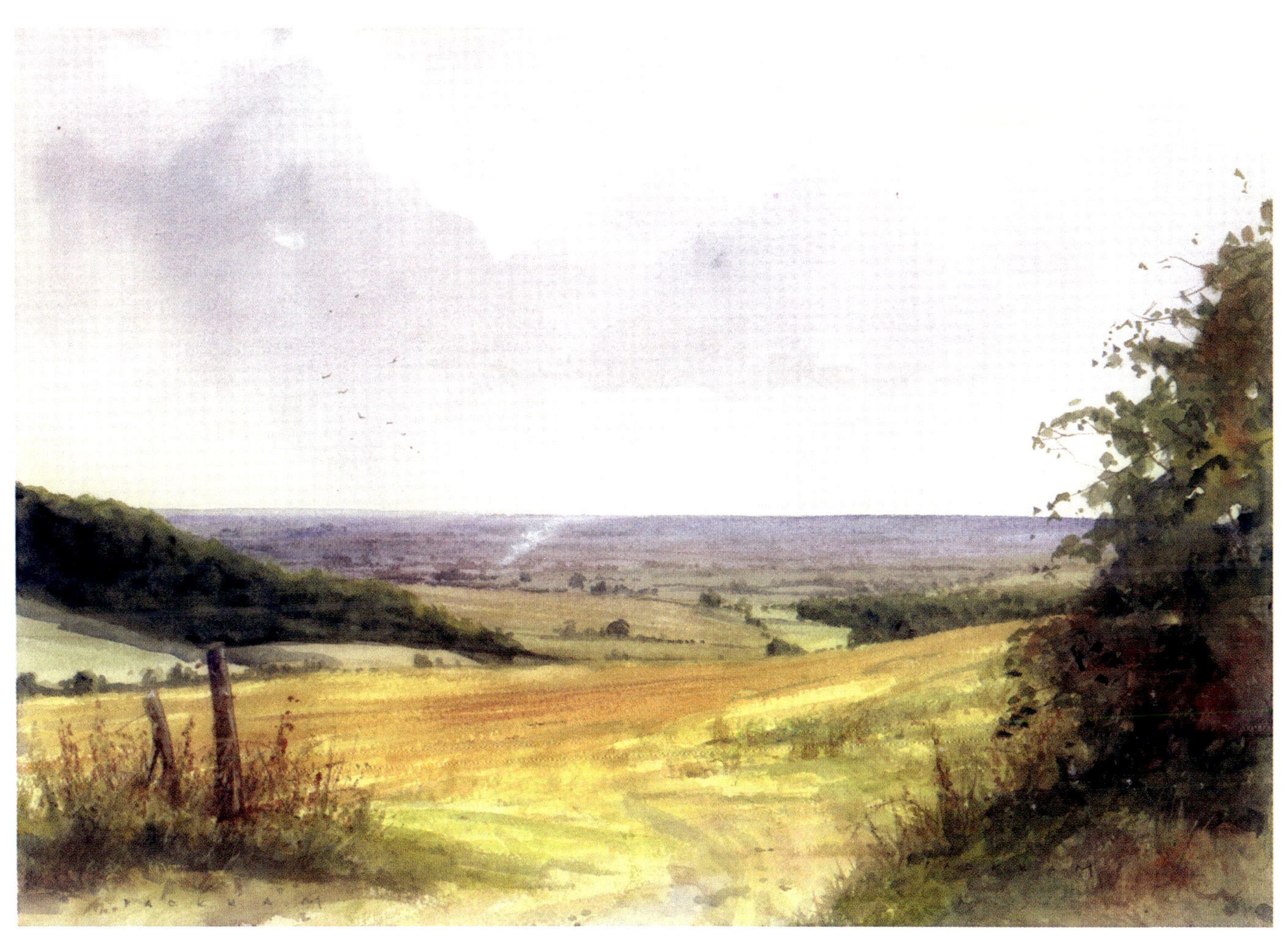

GRENOSIDE

I TRAVEL AT least once every week to Sheffield and on my journey, weather permitting, I take the scenic route which skirts Penistone and Wortley and leads me to Wharncliffe Side to the north east of Sheffield which retains much of its ancient woodland. This view looks west into a setting sun.

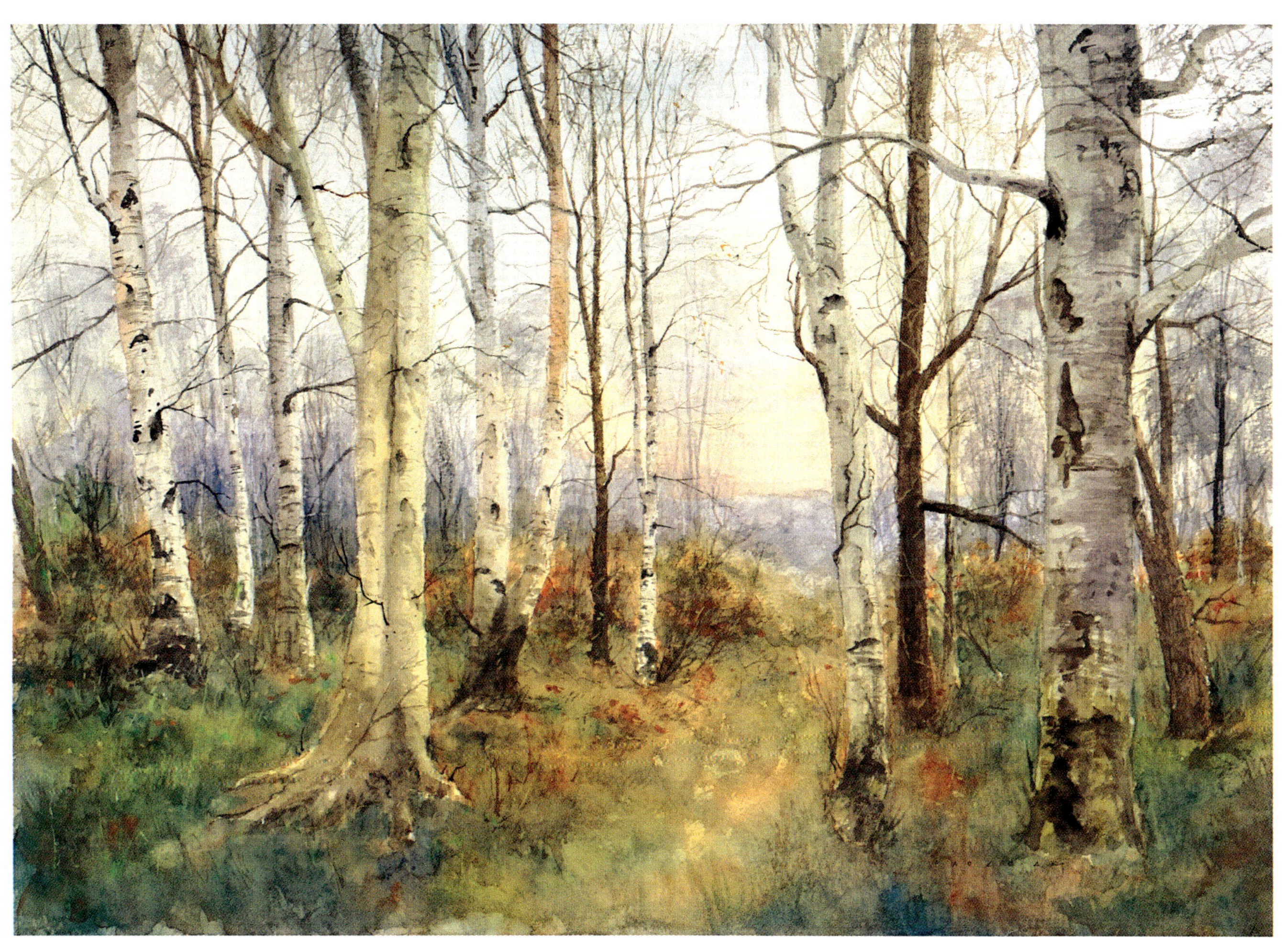

LANGSTROTHDALE CHASE

THIS AREA ONCE belonged to my dear, late friend Graham Watson who bequeathed it to the National Trust several years ago. It therefore holds very special memories for me of this beautiful area and is also a particular favourite of my wife Judith. This view is near the source of the river Wharfe and is typical of the scenery in this location.

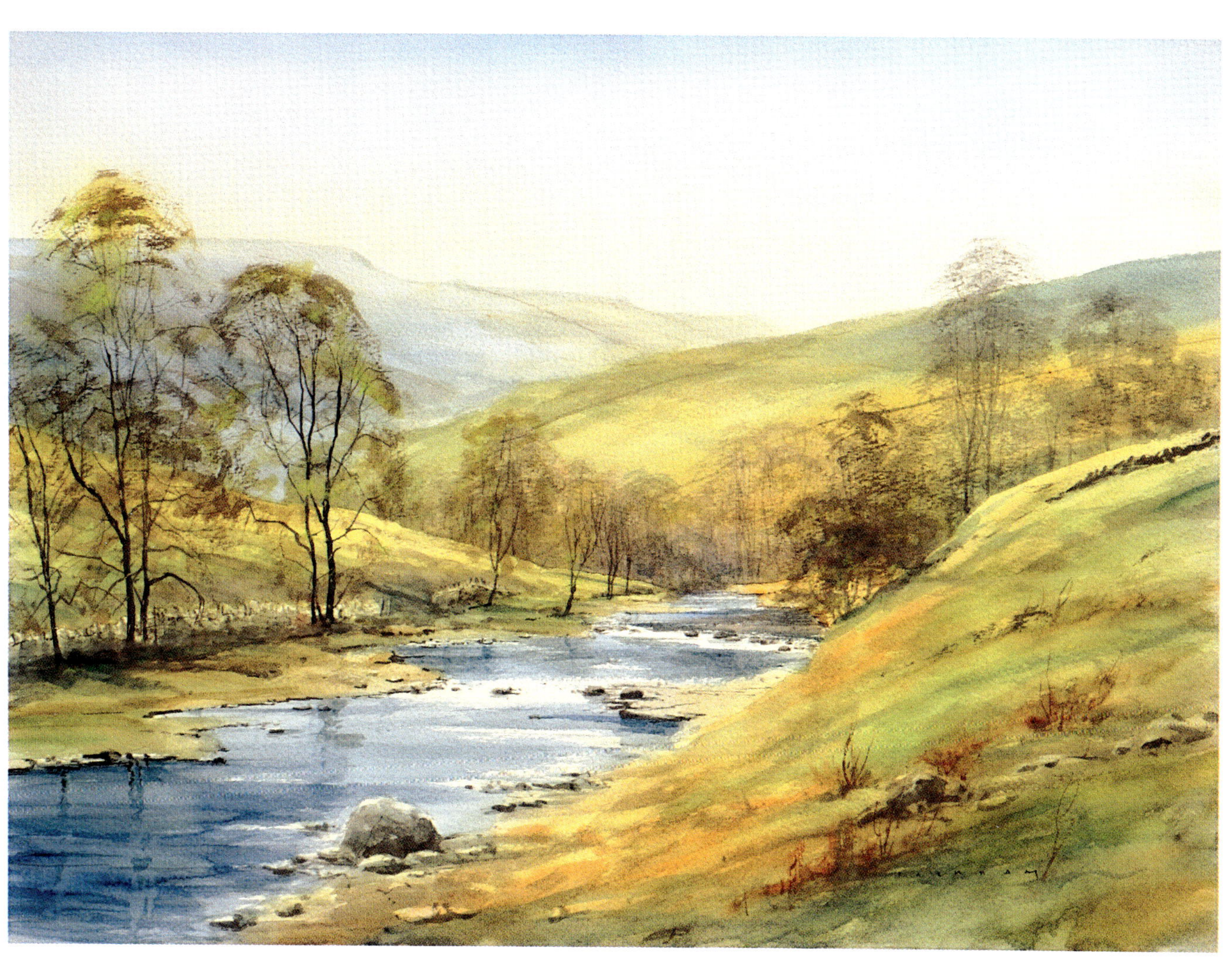

ROSEDALE

I TRAVEL ACROSS the North Yorkshire Moors on a regular basis on my way to Whitby, and I never fail to appreciate the sheer beauty of the vistas provided here. Whatever the time of year, they always seem to yield a good composition for a painting. This picture with the sheep in the foreground and the path leading in to the distance highlights the rugged splendour of the area.

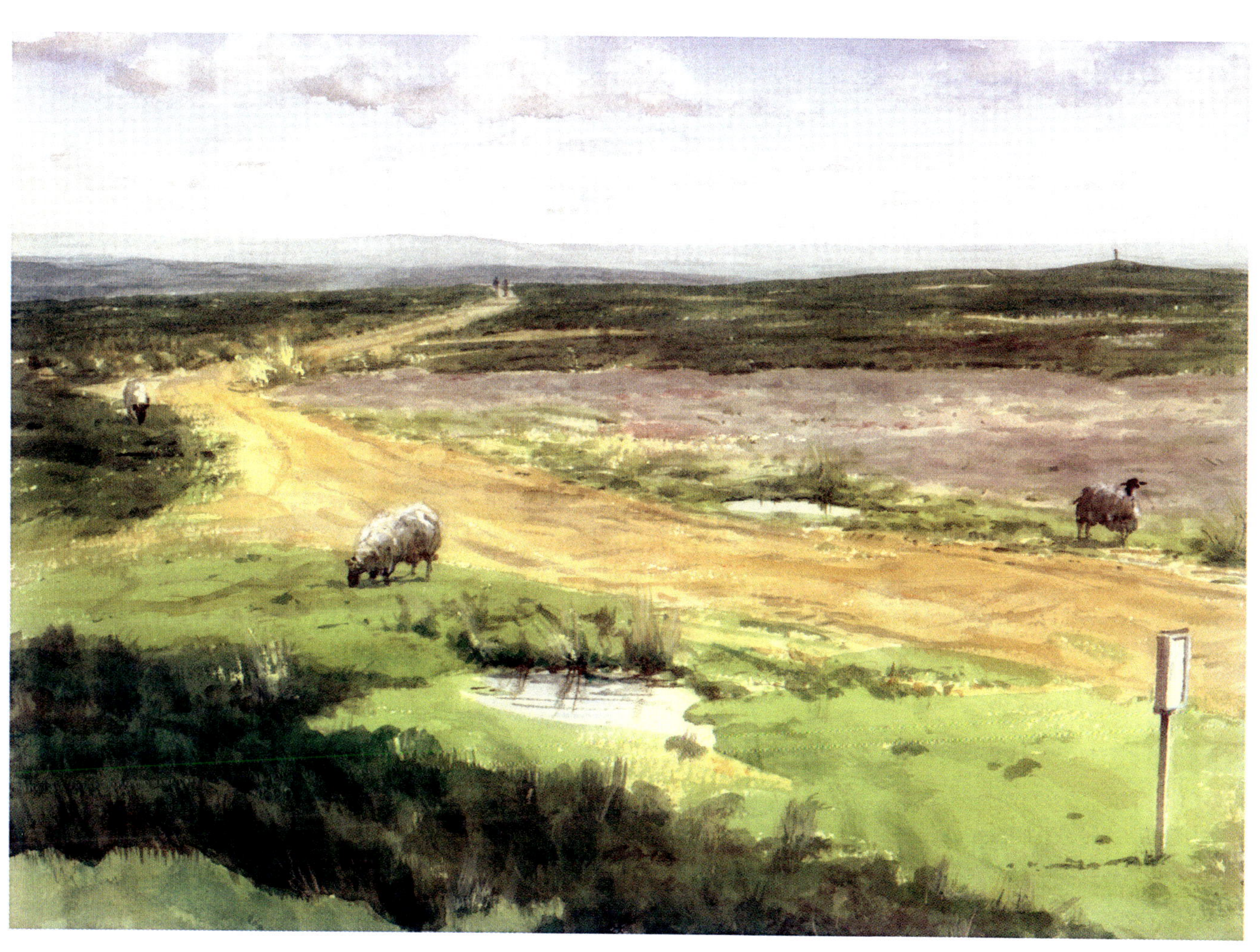

RIEVAULX COTTAGES

I DID AN exhibition with English Heritage at Mount Grace Priory. I then decided to take a closer look at other abbeys in Yorkshire including Rievaulx and was immediately struck by the tranquillity of the surrounding area and could quite understand why the monks had chosen to build their abbey here. I had a good look around and spotted this little cottage nestling peacefully and thought what a good composition it made with the surrounding trees and greenery.

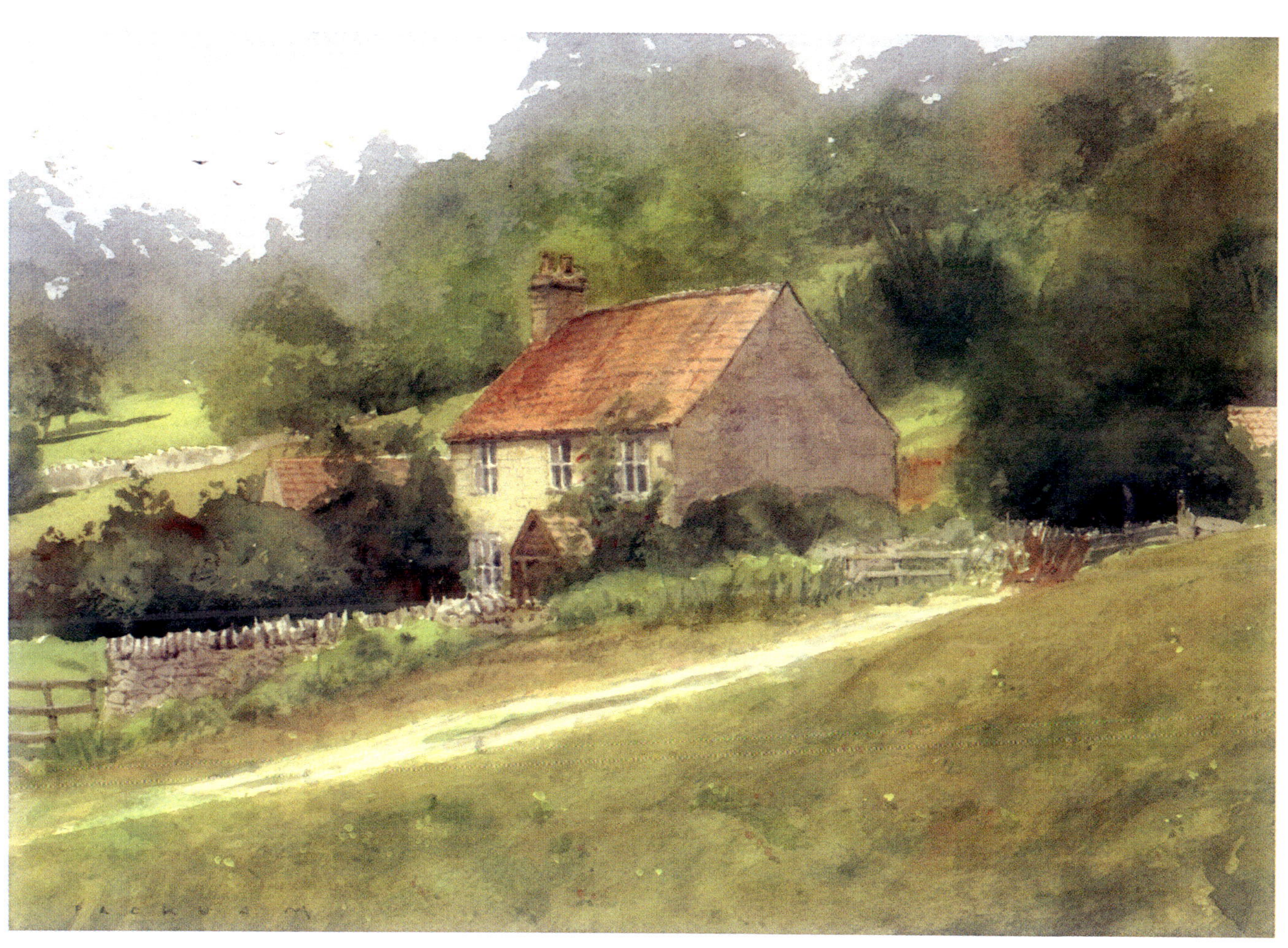

MANKINHOLES

MANKINHOLES IN THE Pennines is the metropolitan borough of Calderdale. This view of a lane leading out of the village provides a starting point for a good walk up to the obelisk known as Stoodley Pike. This 120 foot high monument is a replacement for one built in 1814 to commemorate the end of the Napoleonic wars which was demolished by lightning. The replacement was completed in 1856 and this time signified the end of the Crimean War. It later had a lightning conductor added!

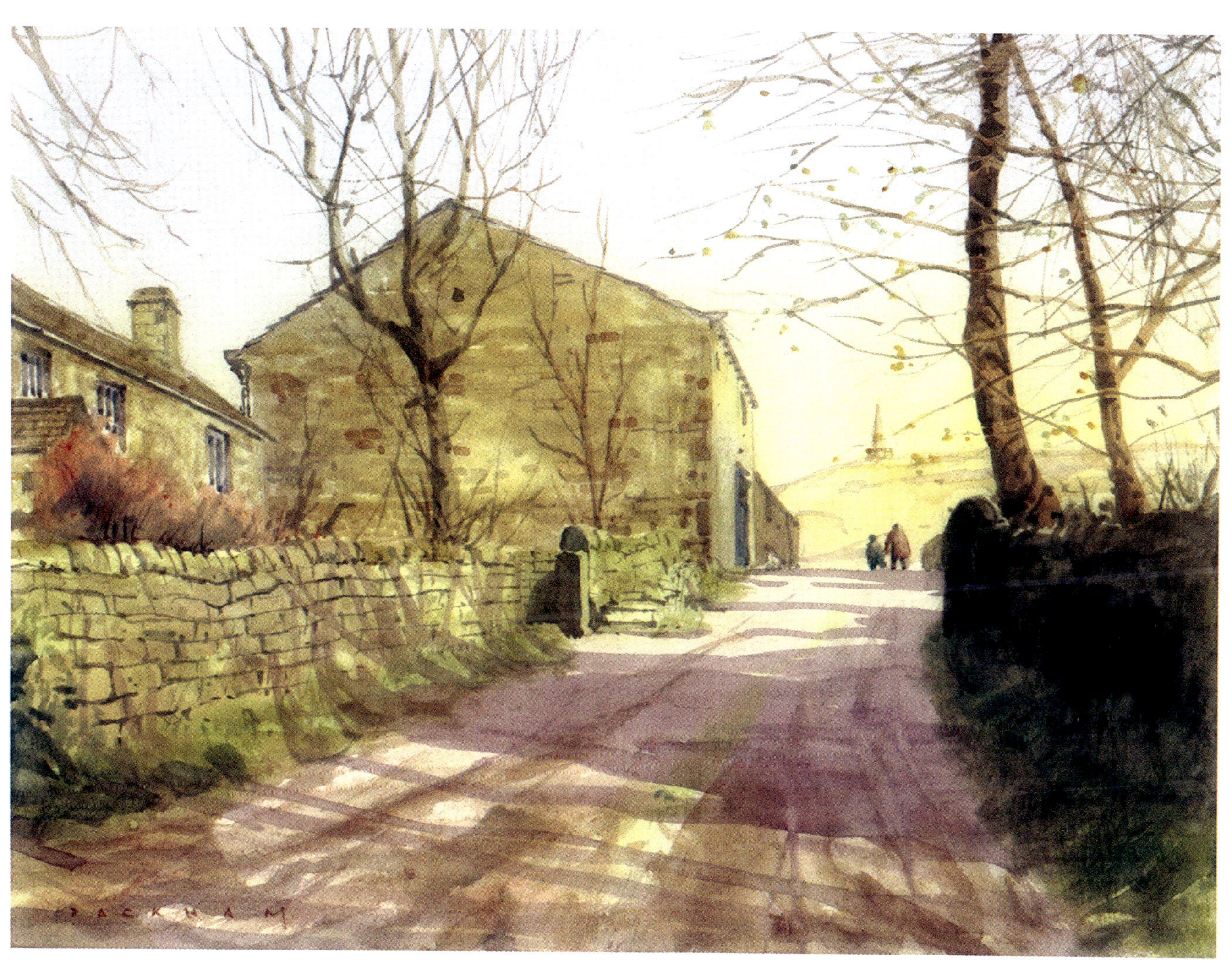

PENISTONE CHURCH

PENISTONE IS A place I often visit on my way to Sheffield and boasts many attractive features. I particularly like this composition of the Church on a late afternoon just as the leaves are beginning to fall and there is an autumnal chill in the air.

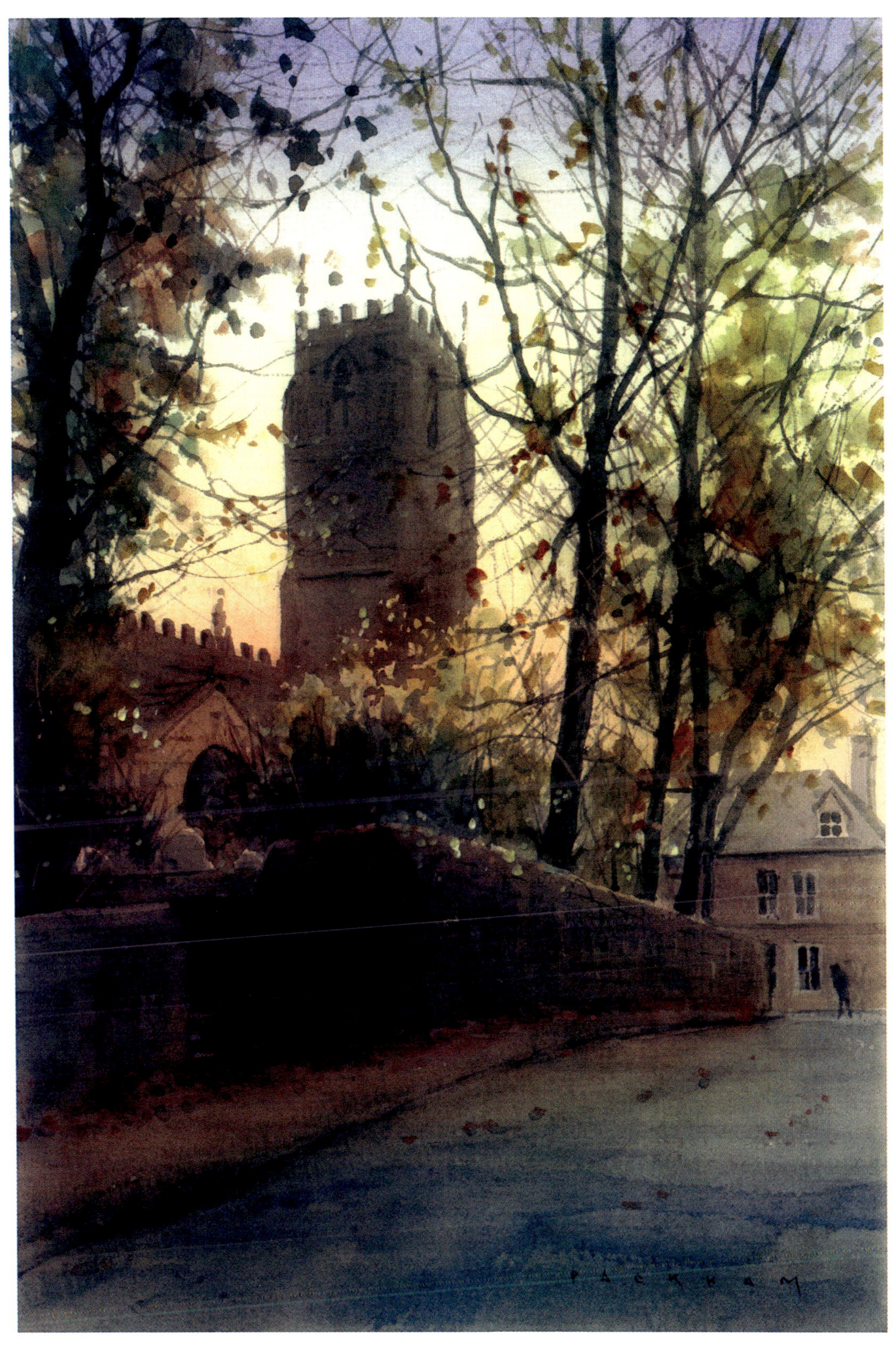

LEEDS
TOWN HALL

LEEDS TOWN HALL is an outstanding example of Victorian architecture which stands proudly in the heart of the city. This is a preparatory sketch done for a much larger commissioned piece of work, however, I feel it still gives the viewer the essence of this magnificent building, as well as an insight into how I approach a painting.

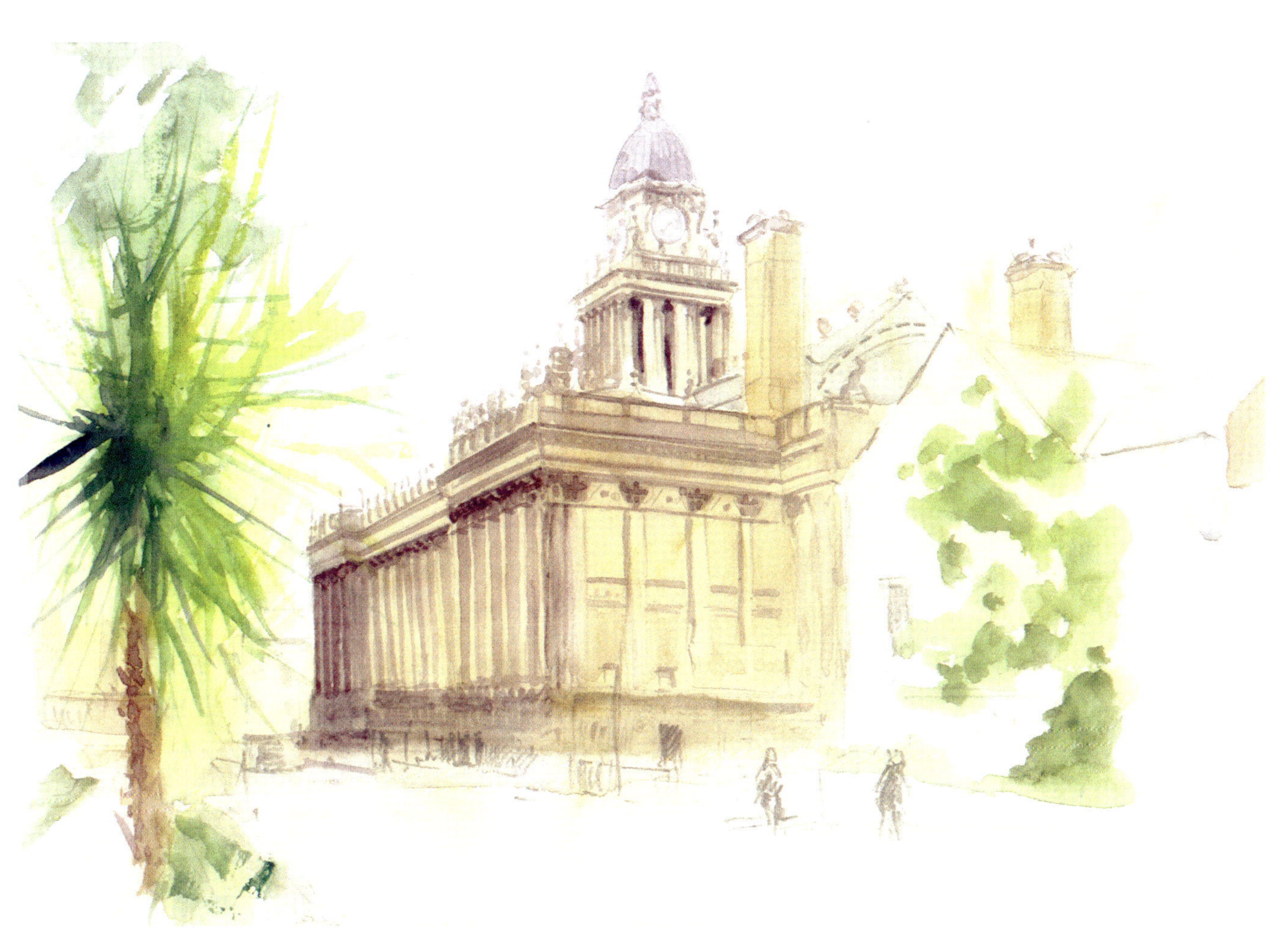

KILNSEY WITH CONISTONE

NO TRIP AROUND the Yorkshire Dales would be complete without a sheep study. I captured this little flock as they were being driven along the river bank at Conistone.

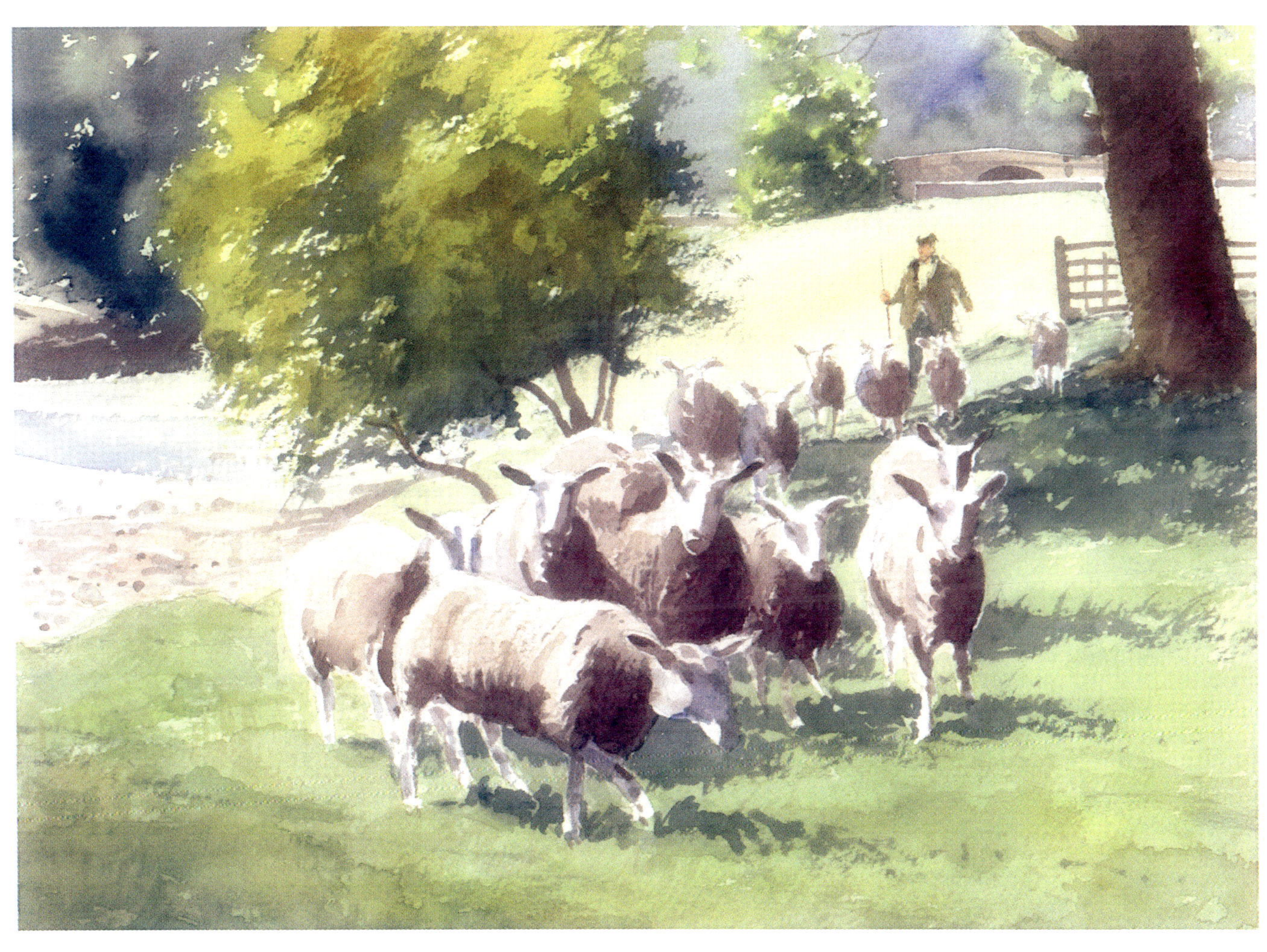

KNARESBOROUGH
AND THE RIVER NIDD

KNARESBOROUGH IS A historic market town about four miles east of Harrogate. The view here is of the railway viaduct and the river Nidd. I painted this view from the castle ramparts in high summer.

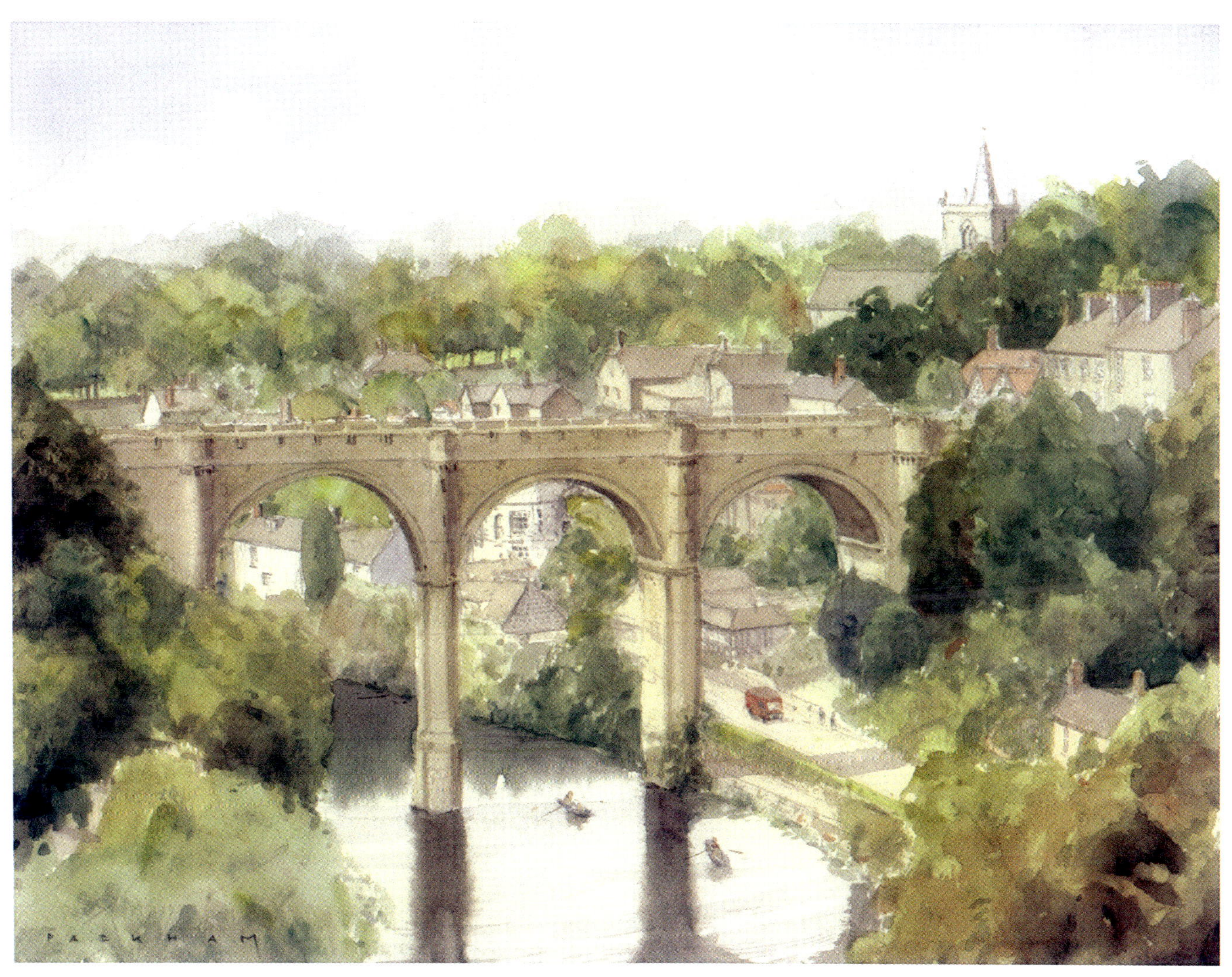
PACKHAM

TADCASTER

TADCASTER IS SITUATED on the river Wharfe between Leeds and York and is a pleasant market town. The bridge painted here was originally built in the 1700s but has been widened twice since that date. As I have previously mentioned, I like bridges and this one is a very fine example, and of course, in the background are the breweries.

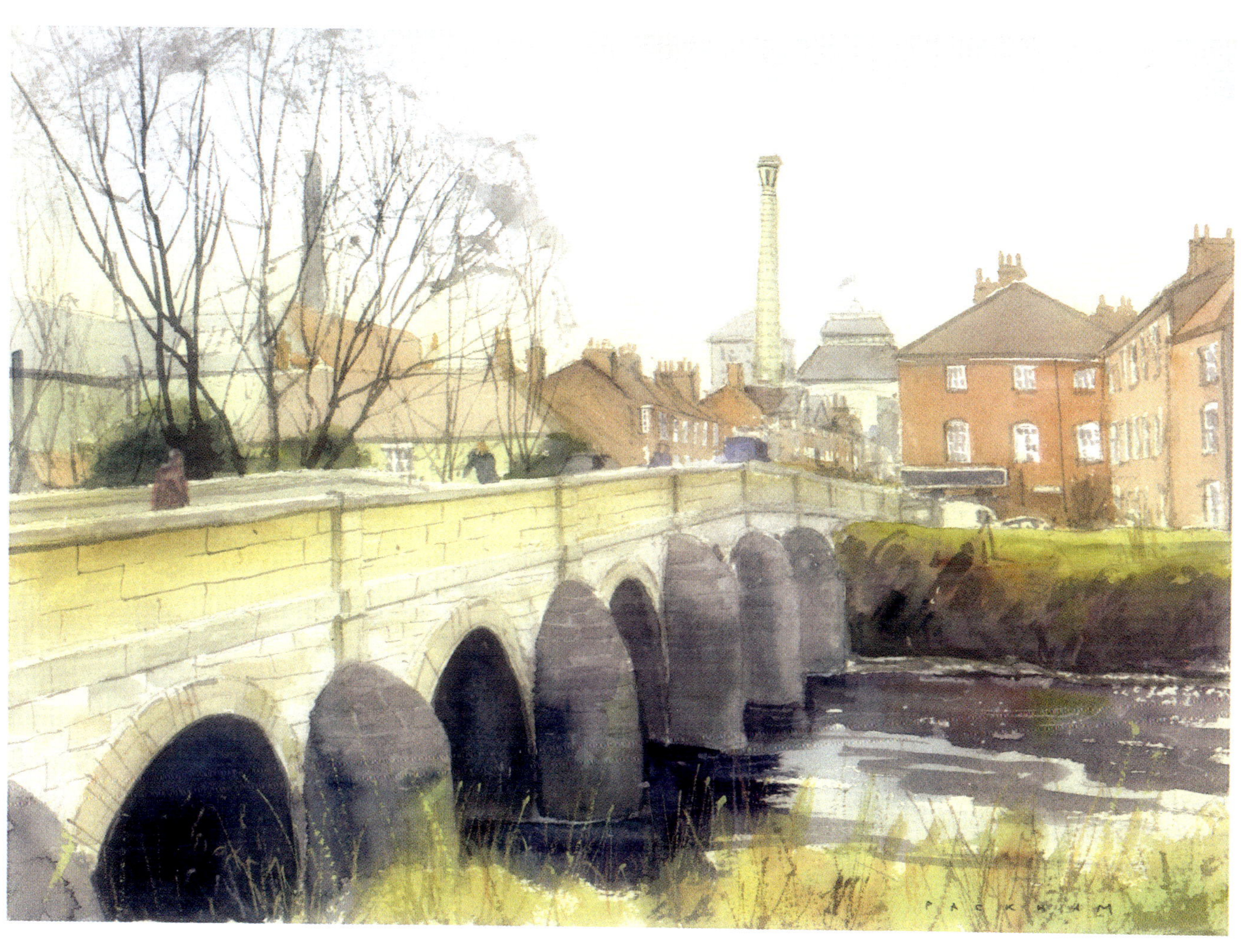
PACKHAM

GREAT OUSEBURN

THE VILLAGE OF Great Ouseburn takes its name from the river Ouse. This composition was completed early in the year just as spring flowers were blooming but before the leaves appeared and masked this particular view.

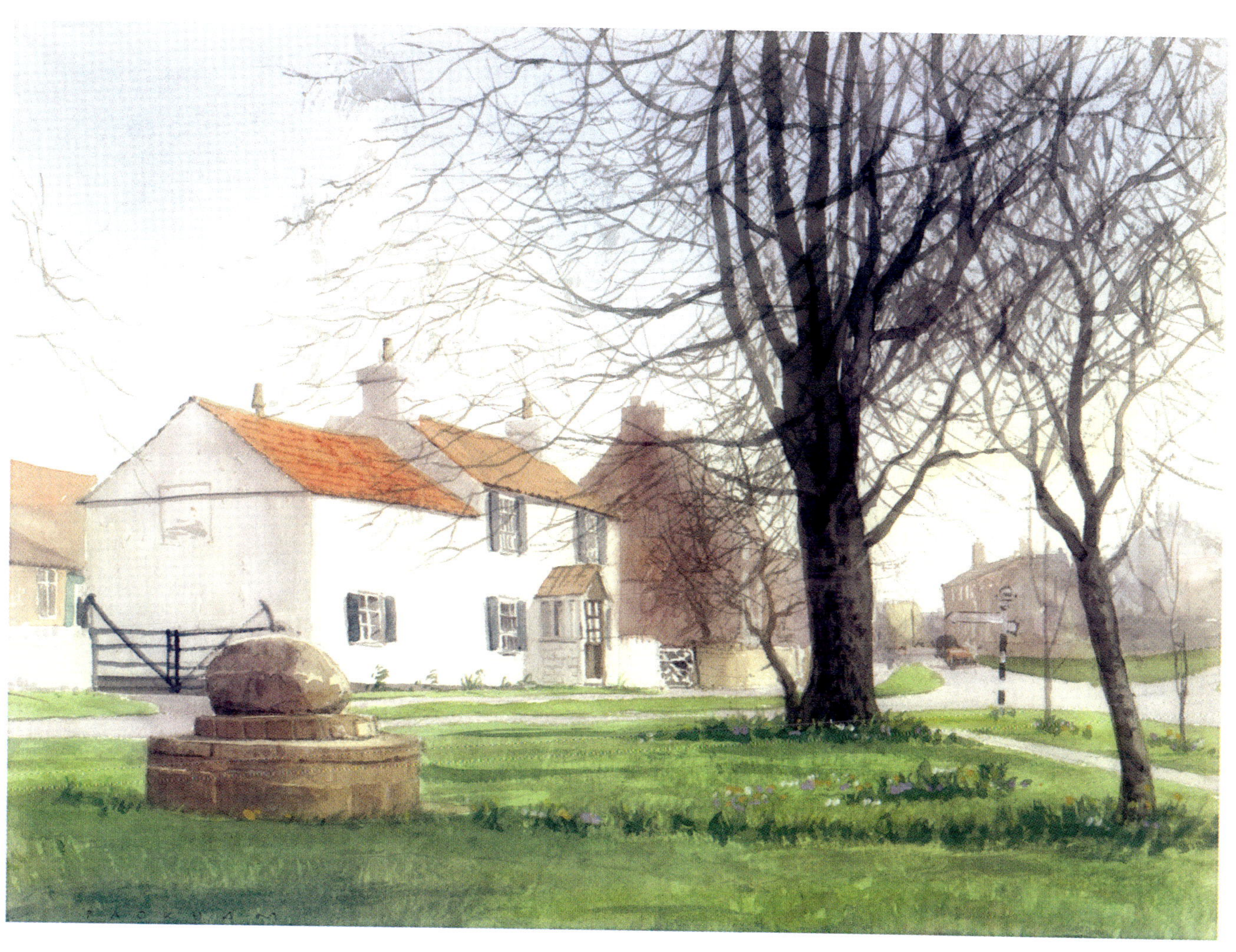

YORK

YORK MINSTER STANDS head and shoulders above the rest of the city and this well known view was painted from the north east. I remember taking an American visitor to a service there and for once in his life he was rendered speechless. Once his speech returned he announced it was the finest building he had ever seen – no argument there then!

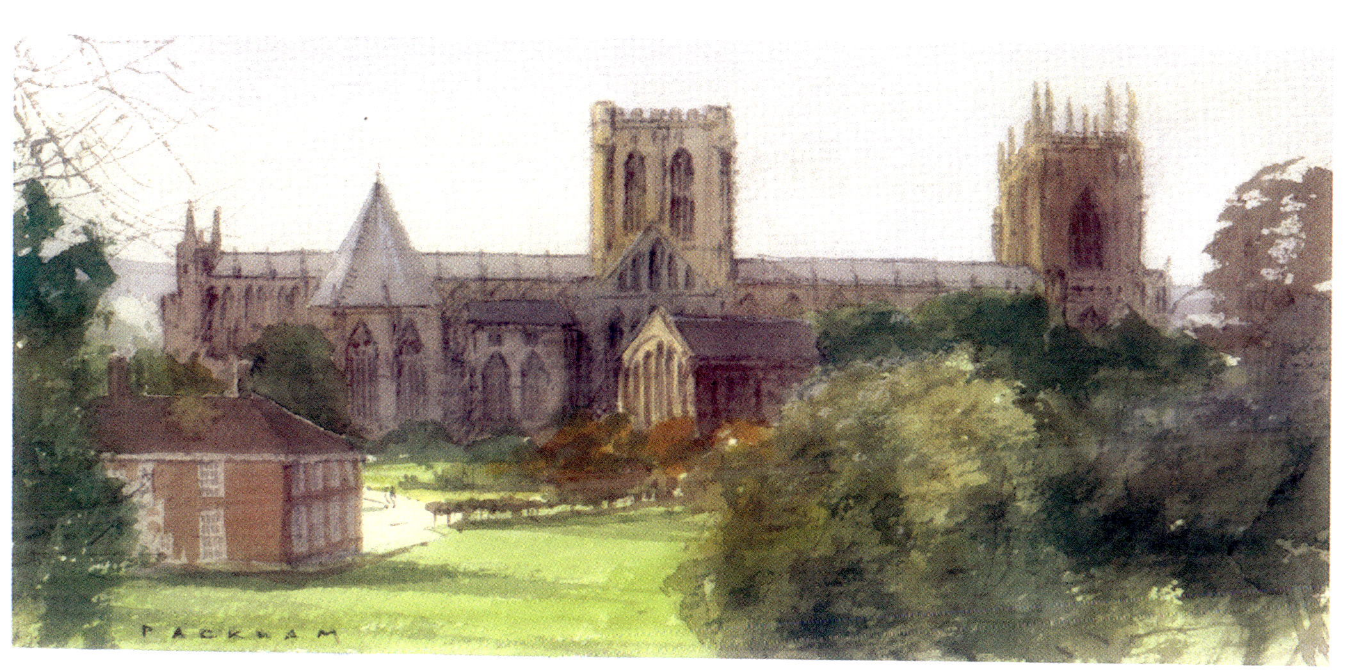
PACKHAM

MIDGLEY

THE SNOW OF winter was just beginning to disappear when I painted this view of woodland close to the village which lies south west of Wakefield.

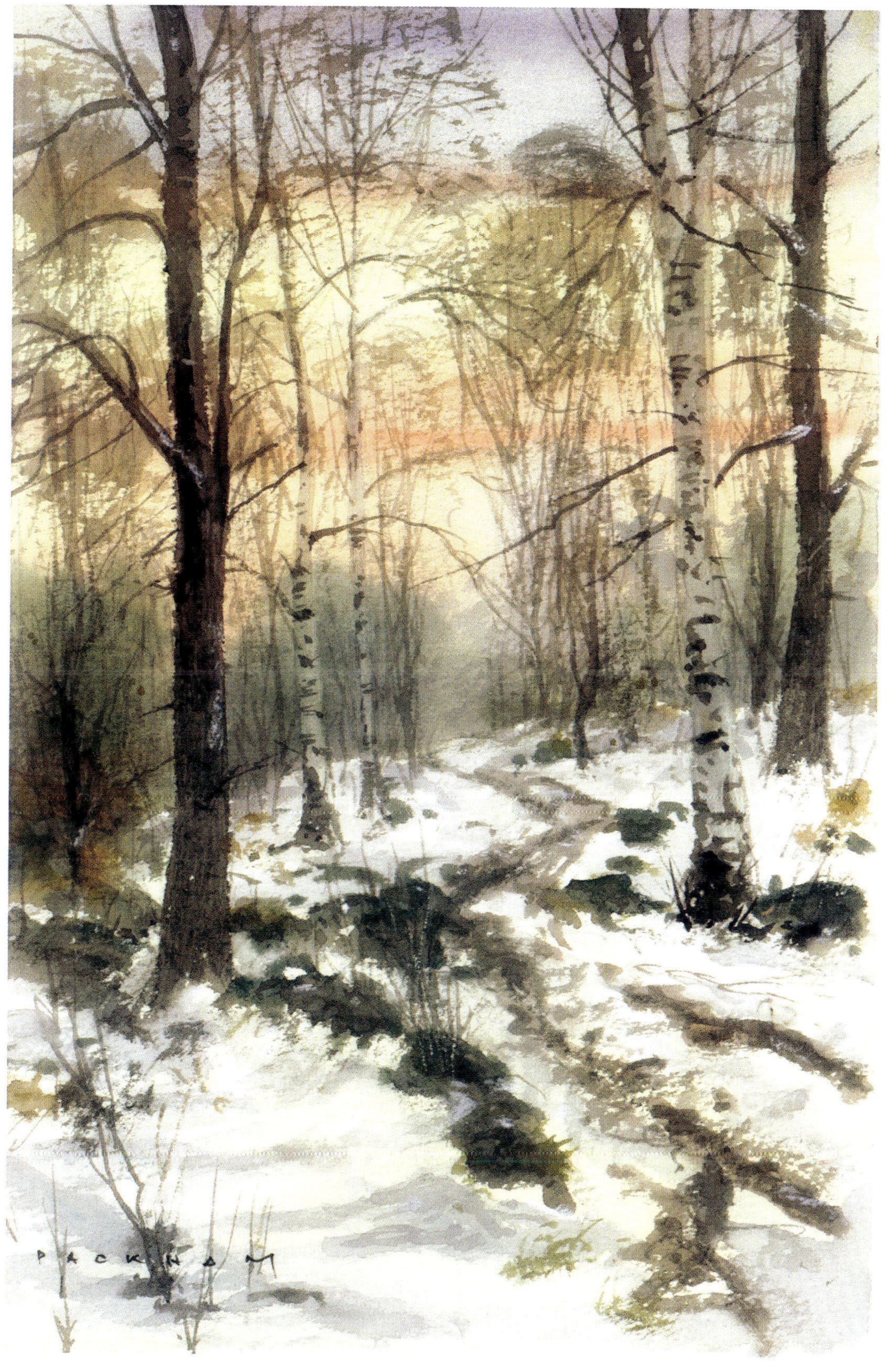
PACKHAM